DEDICATION.

These — unto thee Lord, Life and Love of things,
First leaves and lispings of Thyself in me,
First flashes of that fair self mine to see —
Bring I as one unto his Parent brings
His fledgling offerings.

These same — unto the dear Humanities,
The million-featured God of tongues and times —
Faint echoes of th' everlasting chimes
That were before the Earth-thought did arise,
To fill space with its cries.

Let Sacrifice find out th' holiest shrine,
Beauty, Truth . . or Man-God that shall be :
Their best heart-works men dedicate to ye . .
Light shines through single souls for all to shine —
And this ray shone through mine.

A SONG OF AMERICA, AND MINOR LYRICS,

BY

V. VOLDO.

NEW YORK :
HANSCOM AND COMPANY.
1876.

Press of Wynkoop & Hallenbeck,
113 Fulton Street, N. Y.

That men may fear the less but love the more,
That by love they may rise as seraphs rose,
That fierce unrest may yield to fair repose,
That tranquil trust may see the future shore —
That doubting may be o'er.

Through all in all one law doth knit the ages,
One Love and Wisdom parent all that is . .
By soul-perfecting man shall find his bliss —
The Beautiful shall type his being's pages,
Obedience its stages.

The alter of Old Death — since Time began —
The alter of Young Life with its sweet flowers,
O quaff the incense of angelic hours!
And earlier find in the immortal Plan
When Heaven is shrined in Man!

CONTENTS.

Odes.

Miscellaneous.

SONG OF AMERICA.

CANTO I.

THE UNWRITTEN.

All hail! O Spirit of the magic chord!
Lend of thy fire one spark to thrill my string,
My untried lyre gave by Apollo lord:
Hap'ly and oft in fancy journeying
Have I approached thy evangelic spring
O proud Parnassus, and from the luscious bowl
Drank with a frenzied thirst, sighing to sing—
Come then, glad Nine, ye minstrels of the soul,
Awake each waiting pulse and let your numbers roll.

Canto I.

THE UNWRITTEN.

WHEN Earth was but a fledgling, and her race
First entertained the everlasting space,
And Time began another æons score
To swell the treasures of her vasty store,
A Continent stretched ribbed against the main
Which murmuring Change since ordered to be twain.
Age upon age in patient flight had swept
O'er waking Life and Law that never slept,
Converting atoms to gigantic chains
Of rocky isles, and these to boundless plains,
Upturning all to wear some later form
Mapped by the Fates and moulded by the Storm,
'Till this great change was at the last decreed,
The sister worlds must be forever freed.

A dreadful shudder breaks upon the air—
As of fierce travail for a mightiest heir—

A deep sonorous palpitating sound,
As though a fallen star's far-made rebound,
Or banks of clouds had pierced the quivering sod,
That thunders pent might roar the Will of God—
Broke near and far, re-echoed with a swell,
The mingled cry of Heaven and Earth and Hell . . .
Oh, that the Sea, keen-stinging Lightning's sword,
Had snapped the life-strings ere this awful Word
Both seething Sea and loftiest Land did smite,
To freeze all sense with thrice-destroying fright.

High from her seat the sweeping plain arose,
All seamed and tortured in her widowed woes,
And black fresh gulfs yawned lustily and far . .
The weeping depths of elemental war.

Thus voices strangely terrible awoke,
And souls of flame, to break the landed yoke,
'Till trembled Earth athwart her Fire-king's tread,
Which willed wide Ocean yet a wider bed.

Lo, now most Free ! most glorious estate !
Say what shall be thy lone and mighty Fate ?
Art thou a favorite fond of Heaven's heart,
Cast upon Time to do some wondrous part,

Discover to an Earth immortal youth,
Or teach its races universal Truth?

Alas! thou shalt have travail for thy hire,
And write thy story with red types of fire;
From thine eyes briny tide
Shall thy salt seas be amply re-supplied;
Serpents shall hiss from out thine wayward hair,
And thy false joy find out its true despair;
Thou shalt learn how to live by dying oft,
Then rising, spirit like, from thy dead dust,
Heeding the lore thy being found aloft,
That Love is Life and Death's first name is Lust—
Thou shalt escape the Reaper that is Rust,
And seeing thy sweet goal,
Shall like the Gods become and fill space with thy soul.

See now the young years start
With strained necks down the plain of prophecy,
Each panting for the lustier part
And most astounding immortality—
Nay, candor, fold your weary wings,
Not Lightning's self can catch these headlong things,
As on and on they dart.

But from the vocal bosom of the Wind,
Lo hear ye of these years
Storied in tunes and tears—
And gather flowers and ashes strewn behind.

LURLIN.

O what the broken stories of Love,
O what the lamentings of dead desire,
My face has forgot its cunning to move,
The embers are cold of my vital fire,
For this, mayhap, my wooers have flown,
I have yellow of dust and white of bone,
Fuel for passion's funeral pyre—
Smouldering alone.

ERNA.

Beauty unkempt is a flower of a day,
Tri-colored gloss that fades away
Without the stain of a trace ;
A streak of heated golden light
Caught in an hour by blackened Night—
The myth of an idle chase.

FAULA.

I see at my feet the dregs of a wasted hope,

And the ashes of a joy . .
I lived as a madman who had broken his rope,
And made reason a toy.

GARNET.

My form was chiseled from frozen foam
And warmed by the torch of a star;
My eyes told the tale of a sun-writ tome,
My skin wore the clearness of spar;
The lovers that came bowed low at my feet,
And sung of my smiles and my beauty's conceit
Through day and through day-lighted night;
I sipped the sweets of one short Spring,
Its honeyed woes and delirious sting,
Then saddened the earth by my flight.

* * * * * *

Lo, at the shy beginning of an age,
Another round from the eternal wrung,
Yearning to read the Past's unwritten page —
A poet prayed and sung.

"Howbeit, in truth, thy service has been great
Hesperia, and long of durance, too;

An hundred thousand years of man-estate!
Oh! that some Muse thy wondrous record knew,
Or knowing, would relate,
To the amazement of the bigot crew
That make thy oceans narrow drops of dew.

"And sing thine empire of the Amazon,
Of Lind or Tyne or powerful Strabonne,
Or maratime Larnee
That had ten-thousand sail upon the sea—
Nay start not with thy selfish secret start,
But yield the voiceless burdens of thy heart,
And let us know of thee.

HESPERIA.

The old dark tale of Tyranny and Tears,
The present, pain, the future dumb with fears,
Crouchings and cursings low and deep and strong,
And fierce revolts against the yoke of Wrong;
Dread failings of the weak to win their right,
Dread triumphs of the base to wield their might,
New-robed Alarm arousing here and there,
Winged on a cold, suspicion-poisoned air,
Joy-laden dreams all mocking as they part,
Nor peace nor pride to buoy the hungry heart.

RECORDING ANGEL.

Others sipped of the wise-tree's wine,
And strange knowledges to their finger-tips
Leavened each life-throe as with fire;
And they conversed with gifted Gods,
Or face to face with Deity,
Amidst the lunar porches of the night:
'Till eye-lit and soul-illumined
They conceived God-hood———
———and dared the same!
Becoming as cedars among basil-tufts,
And visioned with the sight of diamonds.

HESPERIA.

Here was a later love — a rich vain mart
Whose name is writ in air,
Whose work and worth is in Eternity—
That test of ev'ry base and better part
And crucible of all things foul or fair;
In truth she was a city gay to see,
With charms voluptuous as the soft South,
With slight sick kisses on her ruby mouth,
On her white neck, and bare,
And shoulders fuller than the moon's round face,
Sharp jeweled teeth found an unchallenged lair,

And in her languid hair
Most idle sighs persued their lazy chase .
Lo, now, a wee red worm is in her place,
For over her despair
Death waived the merest shadow of his hand
And unopposed made conquest of the land.

"Ah, what then of her neighbor cities pray?
Say on — Thou wilt not cease so soon — Oh say,
What of the fierce and feverish Balrook
Who lorded all the Indies with a look,
Whose very throne was propped with edg-ed swords,
Whose law was in the prowess of his hoards?

HESPERIA.

No just ambition woke his low desire
To thoughts of virtue or to deeds of fire,
But like a charred half-statured crumbling trunk,
Apart — as if all beauty from it shrunk —
He stood and died and hid him with no tear
To mark one value of his life's career.

Not so — he held deep in his blighted breast
A secret beauty he had scarce confessed,
And let one good escape guilt's chastening rod

That tiny virtue is a spark of God.
Behold its fruit—though like a flower cave-cased,
Or star-oasis in a desert's waste,
It perfumes all about, and glads and gains,
Leavens the whole through Love's electric veins,
Leads by its light to Glory's anxious goal,
And lends salvation to the coming soul.

TIME.

Oh, bliss of darkness! Luxury to wife!
How hell is ta'en for heaven and death for life!
Pleasure prevails by wanton blindness planned,
Her towers and trophies builded in the sand. .
Fills the poor eye with sheens that fade and fly,
Wraps the wild ear with perjured minstrelsy,
Binds the dead heart with loves that are but hates,
Deserts her victims to their barren fates—
A transient reign of siren-tempting rust,
A form and soul begat of Death and Dust.

RECORDING ANGEL.

Yet see queen Hope a later realm provides. .
Deep as of yore and glad her pregnant tides,
A state more fair, more glorious and strong
For having passed the crucible of wrong;
Wisdom as wide but of a truer health,

Coffers as full but with more worthy wealth,
The new arises where the ancient rose,
With fuller glories and with fewer woes.

"Hail the new lyre — it sings of mastered wrongs,
And sympathy inspires its hallowed songs,
Delves the deep mines of error and of woe,
And where naught else will shine bids Hope to glow;
Directs where Glory shames th' retiring Gloom,
The Light that leads us to, then past the Tomb.

HESPERIA.

But here, alas, a blissful reign to close,
Appears the spoiler War with all his woes,
Complaining drives the charms of Peace away,
And closing hers, begins Disorder's day.

TIME.

Famine and Lust have had their days to live,
And gave their ashes — all they had to give:
Stark Pestilence has ravished state by state
That tardy learned its self-invited fate;
Dishonor, Fraud and Pride that would not bend —
That unopposed are heralds of the end —

War — whose single being was to slay —
Sloth and oppression — each have had his day.

RECORDING ANGEL.

Departed not extinguished is the fire
That made each fibre of this world respire,
Warmed its minutest vein and tiniest cell,
And moved these pulses cold to glow and swell.

CYBELE.

I know for myself that I have been mother to Gods,
And the Mistress of Men,
And have shaken the proud sea and shore with my rods,
And shall shake them again ;
If one be Creator — Creatress am I of the Earth,
The Queen-bearer of Life,
Well knowing the strange and undefined secrets of birth,
Being great Aty's wife ;
I have freighted the hours with wealths of the joy of me,
The sweet prime of my prime,
My Opalia, my warm Megalesia shall be
To the last throe of Time.

* * * * * *

Time, Passion, Lawlessness — akin engage
To make old, new — a youth that still is age —
Ambitious Change vast Empire downward hurls
And bids its atoms bear succeeding worlds.

Behold the plan of wisdom and of God,
The righteous products of a righteous rod,
E'en by decay profoundest ends are wrought.
Experience is the Victory of Thought!
The conquest of the soul, the life of Life,
That grows by proper exercise and strife.

Canto II.

SILENCE.

False life and true are kinships grown apart;
The one is living death — a vague cold sense
Of being when love's health has quit the heart,
And day is darkness and truth, violence;
Th' other is a clear unequal spring whence
Flows a smooth infinity of bliss,
Far swelling with its rich munificence
Of health and light and summer — the arsis
Of the rounding soul and her sweet privilege it is.

Canto II.

SILENCE.

WHY is yon sun so sickly pale and wan —
Hath warmth fled out of it?
Lo, why is Uxmal hushed? mayhap its folk
Have not forever gone!
But what black thing doth sit
Upon its throne in plumes of noxious smoke —
A devil-bird. . or fiend of Curdleroke?
At best he hath a serpent unto wife
That giveth answer with the hiss of hell;
Where hath poor Incense hidden with her spell —
Where the Magician, Life?
Even the air hath taint
Like musty saltless vapor of a tomb;
The strange green'ry has lost its lusty paint,
The flowers have forgot to bloom;
I see now the waters stand stone still!

Is it Sleep's hollow reign,
Th' sullen Sleep of dark mysterious Night?
Lo, frightful shadows sport upon yon hill,
And 'mid the silences their long necks strain
As there were sackcloth harrowing their sight.
Ah, the dumb days and unresponsive nights . .
Ah, white severe mute lips of ev'ry form—
Howbeit they needs must speak unto the storm!
Nay e'en the winds denying their glad flights
Are cold to Speech if Speech herself were warm:

O ye unsocial pines,
Whose withered arms close upon empty space,
Where are your runes and vibratory lines
That whilom chorused rapture to the face
Of fair Hesperia! will ye have no signs
Of joy forevermore — unsocial pines?

How is it that all nature sorroweth —
May it not be that God has held his breath
A little space and Earth but seems in death!

O ponderous Silence;
Austere and most insufferable hush,
The damned tyranny of nothingness . . .

How may the prisoned sense
Break through this marble negative and push
Aside the force that chains it to distress?
List; are those not water sounds upon the air,
Dull, thud-like though they be,
And sluggish as a dead man's heavy hair?
Alas! alas! 'tis light wherewith to see
Only some deeper in the dread expanse,
On to despair, perchance,
As o'er each hollow hill
Echo doth beckon to the lone advance,
Where very sound tells but of silence still.

Sleep! is it sleep — or Winter's withered blank?
Nay, Nature's self is dead;
Gray Spring is sapless as yon barren stone;
Summer has grown sere and lean and lank,
And the red mouths she fed
Have kissed fast to the white dust and white bone.
Sleep! or dead Calm — or awful Rest of things;
A very phantom pause!
Solemn and still and sombre as is Death,
Or Time in weeds courting the worm that clings,
Companioned by the hungry tooth that gnaws,

And stark dry ghosts that wildly sorroweth
That they to ravens gave the cunning of their breath.

O, the lean viands that the grov'ling eat,
And gorge upon, till sickening they turn
And starve with all their fullness : 'tis meet
That so it is — though Nature's bar is stern,
Yet it is just, and many tardy learn
The fatal penalty who gave nor ear,
Nor eye, but chose a desert where to burn
Their torch feasting on bitter clay. . and here
The end — a waste of dust unmoistened by a tear.

There is a smallness in some human shapes
That challenges the microscope though still
As large as Atlas — it is that which rapes
Chaste Honor and sells Manhood for a mill —
Wearing the hood of Virtue but to fill
Its brazen coffers and then turns to brave
The force that served it. . and 'tis nursed until
It breeds destruction in its lie to save,
And finds its nectar, gall — its gain, a slighted grave.

Beneath it true some infinitesimal God
Awaits the ripe'ning of this half-grown crime!

Yet how beneath Humanity! a mere clod
Wasted and wasting on the shores of time;
O, shamefulest grossness! why in the slime
Of Ocean the beast leviathan has an
Nobility, but here bred in a clime
Of energy are shapes of lower clan —
Honored because unknown — he lies who calls them
— Man.

Seek then in vain — amid such heaps of clay —
Such chaff-heaps of man-life there is nor peace,
Nor power nor pleasure for one day. .
Ah, strength roots not in weakness — nor will cease
The burning routine of our dust's decrease,
While flame on flame is fed and ushered on —

Lo! the mad minion rends his little lease!
And when the latest shred of it is gone,
Look where the tortured soul yet dares a master's
throne!

* * * * * *

Nathless how long shall this dead world *be* dead—
Her keen sepulchral chill palsy the air,
And shudder skyward in the name of Dread?

When shall intelligence succeed yon stare,
Color or perfume heavenize the hair
Of yon bowed willow's head?
Mayhap the slight fine feet of mighty God,
Are even now advancing to her heart,
Messaged with His will
That it shall *not* be still,
But rise right upward with magnetic start,
And seek the goal of its triumphal part;
Mayhap the subtle hand of secret God
Bearing the lighted torch of new sweet life,
Doth now illume the sapless whited clod,
Doth now reveal the omnipresent nod,
Directing on the everlasting strife. .
For it was writ before the night was night,
That this Hesperia should not fall — to lie,
Her work unseemly done,
Her race but tenth-way run,
So needful in th' eternal harmony,
And lo, from round to round in Life's unceasing flight
God says — *let there be light* — and there *is* light.

* * * * * *

See, now, the beaming faces of the skies,
The sentiment of love invoked anew!

A-twinkle from ten thousand opening eyes
  Of heavenly brightness nor more bright than true
  To their shy virgin courtship with the dew,
Whose sparkling presence vivifies all earth ;
  Fear not but they'll find place and time to woo,
And bride-chambers that shall have done with dearth,
And marriage-beds where flowers shall spring to birth,
  And clinging tendrils white and pink and blue,
That shall inspire with love and bless with honeyed
    worth.

Announce announce the jubilee,
The chamois horn swell loud and free,
    Waking all drowsy space
    As though a chase
    After new loves found place,
Or an all-shared philitæ
Called to its board of harmony
Generously—joyously.

    Hail unto life re-born !
All hail unto the universal morn !
Th' impatient pines untie their silent tongues,
Canyons conceive the language of their lungs,
The mountain vale, arousing Ocean, sings,
And all the air's a-tinkle as with strings ;

Upon the bosom of a whilom tomb
Luxurious plants and blushing flowers bloom ,
Each, ev'ry grave, a manger hath become,
Where Life doth banish Death and fill his room ,
Bowed forest-giants raise their mournful heads,
Abundant streams resume their empty beds,
The radient heavens, long hidden in the night,
Repeat their panoramas of delight,
And Nature's lusty, longing, lovely arms,
Enfold a million babes a-nestle mid her charms.

Yea, steal away thou sapless Sythe, and lame,
Thou hast become the omnipresent shame,
Youth hath usurped thy unemploy-ed place,
And dares renew the empire of a race.

* * * * * *

This — the glad round of passion and of man —
Great Mind begat of Matter that is great —
Catastrophy and travail and the ban,
Magnificent desires that laugh at fate,
The sublime energy,
The growth and glory of Mankind's *to be*. . .
O kiss the two-edged knife,
And rise superior to thy suffering-hood !
Not length of days but use of days is life,
The wrath of things evolved to Peace and Good

Canto III.

THE RED-RACE.

Now pause upon the ocean-bounded plain,
This antiquated sepulcher of man,
That bursts and blooms with luscious life again
As though its fertile page had just began ;
No mortal mind can multiply its span ;
Like to a plant that mounts a mouldered pile,
And growing, girds and hides the parent plan,
So youth upon this nerveless world doth smile,
And Winter hides his face neath Spring's o'erflowing Nile.

Canto III.

THE RED-RACE.

O BOUNTEOUS-bosomed Mother, God in form,
The loud seas rejoice in thee and the warm
Sky bends over thee with benedictions ;
Thou art the joy of yonder king of suns,
And lusty voices sing thy beauty's praise ;
Bear on the generous glory of thy ways,
The glad fecundity of life, joyous and strong,
A spring-queened age of blissfulness and song.

Lo, on the breast of this exuberant tide —
This mother-hood repeated in the Bride —
Behold a rank outgrowth of human-kind,
A higher body and a happier mind ;
Of whom asked these the privilege to be,
Of whom th' eternal birth-right to be free,

The lightning and the waves for childhood's toys,
Of whom a manhood of sublimest joys?
As though fair Ocean joined in amorous strife
To flood the forests with excess of life,
A mighty race sprang forth as in a night
To witness an existence of delight,
And swell the endless peopling of the skies,
With simplest forms of God's humanities.

How fragrant then these forests far and near,
With a fresh fragrance and a youthful cheer;
The lordly beast, aglow with lusty fire,
Sought undisturbed his cave or jungle-lair,
And only tried his else untested strength
On some kin-king or serpent's ropy length;
Swift flowed the streams unstaid by dam or pier,
Loud shrieked the birds upon their wild career,
New was the day from sun to sleepless sea,
The vital day of Freedom's jubilee.

Then the red native — monarch of his state —
Unmindful of Refinement or of Fate,
Roamed his rich empire with heroic strides,
Joyed in her storms and stemmed her quickest tides,
Dared the vast lakes when fearfulest their flow,

Pursued the bear and savage buffalo,
With springing feet unwound the fatal trail,
'Till foe on foe outpoured his arrowy hail,
Found sweet content in all the rude array,
And gloried in his undisputed sway.

What man shall know the measure of their ways,
What tell the splendid numbers of their days?
Their races came and went
Like spring-time grasses for a season lent,
Save now a stronger populate appears,
And braves destruction for a thousand years.

Oh! guess not what fair altitudes they won,
Nor how some souls may have outshone the sun
How many Hiawathas rose and taught,
And kinged their age in majesty of thought;
What wise Chiabos wrung a golden trace
Of endless life from Nature's living face,
And found in her, when rightly understood,
The vital touch and ministry of God.

It were a sweet communion that, and near —
Their bosoms held no lodging-place for fear,
And could be only moved and did but move
Responsive to some eloquence of Love. .

From th' grand volume of a torrent's speech,
To a frail birdling's silken trembling reach,
Learned they to catch the syllables of Peace,
Earth's present bliss and happiest release ;
With patient vision trained to scenes of power,
The sky's effulgence and the prairie's flower,
Found they delights that would not, could not die,
More infinite than prairie or than sky,
And yet so near — attentive to each grief —
Their Spirit-God loved them in ev'ry leaf.

Nay, let us not, that swell life's later throng,
Familiar with the polished arts of Wrong,
Because their fading shadow scarce survives,
Deny them greatness in their proper lives ;
Alas, they might prove judges of *our* part,
And Nature true rebuke distorted Art,
Declare to us in tones assured and strong,
That sweet Life treads her better way along,
Where man's delight is in his patient gaze
At Nature's works and beauty-quickened ways,
His happiness less in his boastful toys
Than in a simple round of lawful joys,
Aye, in the *being* brave and proud and great,
Less in the place than nature of his state.

Greeting to them that understood the Law,
And read God's pages without fleck or flaw ;
To them less blessed and who, degenerate grown,
Failed to preserve the harvests that were sown,
Who half perceived the Truth, and did it not,
Most bitter pity for their fallen lot. . .
Ah, these shall not resist the whited foe,
Nor separate his Wisdom from his Woe,
Nor harmonize with anything that's his —
But shall succumb unto the Man *that is*,
And to the silences their frail steps wend,
The weary standard-bearers of the End.

Canto IV.

COLUMBIA.

Sweet morning broke with an exultant joy,
And Nature put her richest livery on;
The less'ning stars did with the sunbeams toy,
And glad the earth as in his fullness shone
The gold-king of the day: it was the dawn
Of life as well as light — of happy life —
For birds and beasts and brooks did rapture don,
Summit and vale with vocal glees were rife,
And mid such gracious stars what time for gloom or strife?

Canto IV.

COLUMBIA.

WHAT splendid thing is the theme
Of mariners over the sea. . .
Is it fairy-enchantment or dream,
Or precious miraculous gleam
Of a new maiden-savior to be?
But none of all eyes that had seen,
Perceived her full stature or mein. .
Some saw but the sweep of her hair,
As she flashed through the tremulous air,
As she fled like an arrow of fire.
Others caught sounds — as a lyre,
And some heard the one word — *dare.*
One said. . "In the solemn bleak night,
Bound by a tyrannous fright,
Her hand grappled hold of the reins,
And loosed ev'ry chain of our chains;"

Then said another, aghast,
"Deep in the deep sea's waste,
When by the wild skies tossed
Ocean cried out as if lost!
I saw this same wonderful form
Borne in the arms of the storm,
And laugh with a shrill thrilling glee
Over wrath of the sky and the sea."

Howbeit some ships cast abroad
With faint and irresolute helm,
And doubts that did nigh overwhelm,
'Mid blank barren searchings for God. .
Saw this Token flash forth from the sky,
And without asking whither nor why —
Since surely a Pilot was given
As the Sign of the pleasure of Heaven —
Strained on like glad hounds through the deep
In the wake of the star-lighted leap.

And she led them — this Pilot of God —
To a strand where foot never trod
Whose heel smiteth body or soul. .
Or daring to type its foul tread,
Had died with the things that were dead,

Or blended with death in the scroll
That Life had since worshiped and wed,
And won to immortal control.

And lo, everywhere! everywhere!
Upon the magniloquent shore,
With its boiling and coiling and roar
Upon the weird wings of the air,
Afar on the precipice bare,
Or near on the rock-broken sod,
This presence discovered her trace
Like a smile from a heavenly face,
As the land were her darling abode;
And secure in a Genius of might,
In a Guardian-Goddess-of-Light,
The band grappled hard to the strife
That prophesied Glory and Life!

Ah, now, shall these build a race
And parent the New World's plains?
Aye, fearling, these same by the grace
Of the red sterling health in their veins,
And the force that is writ in their face. . .
There are, among Earth's mankind,
Some souls that a chain cannot bind. .

Some souls so untempted by pelf,
Some heroes so emptied of self,
That they break from their lives' narrow pen
And dare a new blessing for men,
Nor ask of what part *they* will share,
If happ'ly they do what they dare.

Such were the Spartan-bred few,
Inspired with the gift to be true,
  And waiting the gift to be free,
Here armed in the House of the Blue
  In common with sea and with sea.

One morning — some fierce days after —
With joy and with merry sweet laughter,
The sun — and with wandering ken —
Beheld this new order of men,
And the work their strong hands found to do :
'Twas a sight most impressive to view . .
They had dragged the wild brute from his lair
  And taught him to crouch at their feet ;
They had torn up the rocks black and bare,
  And planted their furrows with wheat ;
They converted the tortuous coasts

To havens of smooth sure rest;
Had driven the red forest hosts
To the arms of the infinite West;
On the breasts of the young Thirteen,
Strange charms and new graces were seen —
The wilderness fled with the wind,
And the beautiful sovereignty — Mind —
Succeeded the reign of the Night
With auroras of love and of light.

We will see now what people is this,
Whether made of the earth or the sky —

The hours came forth with a cry
That was born in Oppression's abyss. .
"Lo here is a yoke for your neck —
That till now hath no sign of a fleck —
Here are some gyves for your feet,
And here some fresh wormwood to eat:
They were typed and made at the forge
That is Kinged by the English George,
And here are his lictors in red,
Sent to order the work of his head,
And cunning wrought out by his hand,
Through the height and the depth of your land.

Then ten-thousand voices as one
Made reply to this thing that was done. .
"We are men that for Conscience' sake
Were compelled to give o'er and to break
With the whole painted love of the world;
In dear Freedom's name we were hurled
Upon Ocean's tumultuous breast
To this gem of hers shrined in the West;
But we found on the rough welcome coast
The delights that our bosoms love most;
Found in forests fresh-scented and wild,
In mountains of strength newly piled,
In sweets of a generous soil,
In the health and the culture of toil,
With none to molest or annoy,
A peace and contentment and joy
We never had tasted before,
Nor dreamed it were even in store.

"No man have we wronged in this thing,
Neither Bishop nor Sultan nor King;
We withdrew from the light of the throne,
And rather chose darkness alone;
To find out in silence, apart,
The tie 'twixt our God and our heart.

"Think not we will suffer again
The meanness and danger of men;
We have learned to obey and deny,
We have learned, too, to live and to die;
We've forgot to be mute in our choice,
Our virtues now speak in our voice,
O pure and sonorous and free,
As the story that leaps from the sea.

"We will yield not this fill of our needs,
This asylum of ours and our seeds,
To any that live while we live;
Self-truth is no gift we can give,
And no Master in all of Life's van
Is so great as a self-mastered Man,
Or fitter to rule his own charge,
Though e'en he were Three times a George."

Herewith were these Pioneers smote —
And from many a brown lusty throat
That late made its honest acclaim,
There issued a red liquid flame,
That like Ætna a-leaping on high,
Told its story to earth and to sky,
And stirred the whole sensitive land;

And lo, it arose heart in hand,
'Rose from hilltop and valley and plain,
Quick with courage and muscle and brain,
Unmindful of station or caste,
Singly fired by the present and past,
Singly bent on defeating a fate
That was kindred to Hell and to Hate.

Ah, now what a day was begun
With thy red dawn, O brave Lexington —
It needs was a miracle-morn
That saw a Republican born
Who would challenge the crowns of all Earth ;
A day with a gory fierce girth,
Whose moments were battles of pain,
Each breaking a link of a chain.

No Patriot tardy or lax
  In the glorious work to be done ;
When an ag-ed one fell in his tracks
  His place was re-filled by his son ;
In the homestead, or hamlet or hall,
  Firm women did other than toy,
The wife armed her husband, her all,
  The mother her brave only boy.

Oh, the struggle unequal and long,
Where weakness finds out it is strong ;
In the name of a solemn sweet cause,
These few dare the iron awful jaws
Of an Hydra — to slay or be slain ;
Every nerve is put forth to the strain
With a confidence brooking no rod,
As the work were commissioned of God ;
With a nourishing spiriting trust,
That Triumph was true to the just,
And giants of sucklings are made
When Right crieth upward for aid.

* * * * * *

O what can withstand the flash
From the Divine soul-lash
That lights the mountain to its flinty core ;
What still the interminable roar
That thunders the ubiquitous I Am. .
What woo the Lion subject to the Lamb,
From one shore to the other shore?

O, vain to oppose, O despair!
When there is that in the air

That maketh heroes of the very dead!
The dead that die unto life,
That take sweet Victory to wife,
Becoming glorious in the thing they wed.

As for the quick, lo, here is Washington,
With his brave hand a thousand years upon,
Standing as that stands which is a Sun.

Melt ye the rock-hills into waters blue,
Or stay the eternal tear-drops of white dew,
Or hide the colors of the warm sky's smile;
But think ye not meanwhile
To cleave or quench or kill this spirit born,
Or make Night pall the genius of this Morn,
Cutting Man off from all of him that's true.

For Man so moved apace,
And filled with God-hood to the burning brim,
Will sicken and wear out stupendous space,
Appall Olympus with the ghost of him,
Forgeting not to vivify his place.

I see now that Triumph must be,
Nay that he is
With all Coumbia his,

Wrested from the torment of the sea. .
And the prairies cry *it was our prophecy!*
And the lakes reply, *it was our ministry!*
And Freedom sings, *it is my Glory!*

* * * * * *

Hail to this thing that is born!
Hail to the Herald of morn!
All hail unto her who hath borne
The darlingest gem Time hath worn
In the innermost shrine of his heart!
Oh, stay! thou and we cannot part!
Art thou not crowned as with light,
Thy forehead star-jeweled and white,
Are not many balms in thy breast,
Thine arms full of rapture and rest,
Who fitter than thou for a wife,
That art the Aurora of Life?

And now adown the current of glad years,
Aglow and wonderful as a comet's train,
The new great race appears;
The steam-horse plows the everlasting plain,
And golden lusty grain
Doth wave beside the mountains' golden tears.

And, lo, a splendid Mind-burst spreads its light
  O'er the immortal Monarchy of Man —
  The sober, lawful privilege began
To solve the sacred mystery of Might,
    And make it clean and white.

Canto V.

TO-MORROW.

Life, and its to be — an abundant theme,
Mankind's best contemplation and a thing
Of awful force. Who calls its span a dream,
An idle bubble which a boy might fling
Upon the air to see the vacant ring
It makes when it has fallen, and is not?
Ah, if an atom boasts its joy or sting,
What of the Soul — can it, too, rule then rot?
Eternity it is from whence it was begot!

Canto V.

TO-MORROW.

AH! how canst thou endure, fair thing,
Nay not endure, but how with us abide
Alway as now, our unexampled bride,
Our Hope, our Goddess of incarnate Spring,
Our most and dearest of all gifts beside?

By the soul-training of gigantic men,
And love of women dowered with thy love,
And with the graces that are born thereof;
Whose common bliss will be thy praise as when
Of old the heart leapt up at sight of thee,
And men rejoiced to kiss thy charm-ed feet. .
By greatness forth sprung from the light of thee
Nurtured by principle, more holy sweet
Than, in one drop, all spoils of luxury. .
In hearts of heroes won shalt thou abide,

That brave all toils of hungry Sacrifice
With ready grace for thee they deified;
That choose thy worship at their being's price;
That seek thy feet for better or for worse,
And dare confront a blessing or a curse. .

By that substantial greatness shalt thou live
And is made great wherewith its Cause is great,
Charging with God-hood gifts that it does give
To them that pledge their whole rich soul's estate.

Them that hide self in Truth's or Duty's name,
Will find reward more sweet than wealth or fame,
Here and beyond where, like good seeds well sown,
Good works, more glorious and prolific grown,
Await their doer, the new Cause that is,
With usury of blessings and of bliss.

And in what school shall men learn to be great,
Quick to their country's immortality,
And the grand schemes that shall exalt mankind?
Oh, if the Past be dark and desolate,
If it refused the sight best made to see,
If in their violence blind
Peoples and crowns sowed whirlwinds to the wind,

And each in his own time laid down and died —
Where find the vital life that will abide . .
The Faith, the Truth, the Love, the Hardihood,
The good whose very pleasure is in good . .
That shall grow firmly rooted and secure,
God-tutored in the cunning to endure —
Say, in what school shall men learn to be great,
And challenge e'en the tyranny of Fate?

Look ye! arise! and with uncovered head
And feet of sandals shorn and mute mouth fed
With humble and unutterable awe,
Go forth before the majesty of Law!
The Form, the Soul, the Unity of God!
Seek ye his inner Presence and Abode,
The closets of th' eternal Reasoner!
And there find out the use for which ye were . . .

And howin to be happy in that use,
How to unlearn your habits of abuse,
How harmonize the everlasting Plan,
How to be woman, how, forsooth, be Man!

Now let us ponder boldly — he is mad
Who doth enslave the free estate of thought

Letting the have be but the might have had.
Earth, space, all life is with religion fraught,
Perfect as God, that is not truly taught
By blind interpreters — grasp it and fill
As *thou* dost hunger for what is rightly sought,
Shall all be found, and shall supremely still
The else unanswered wish and unobedient will.

Each fragile leaf, bud, flower, tells a tale
That not in all the creeds of Time is found!
Where is the bigot who will dare assail?
Love, Cleanliness, Obedience — the round
Of bless-ed means — and above all is crowned
The Truth of all, thanksgiving on each tongue,
That swells Creation's glorious resound,
As there were volumes in each tiny lung
Leaping to pour their floods of praises deep and young.

* * * * *

Pause ye apace, for lo, what power is this —
What ocean spills her waters from her lap,
And casts them howling o'er yon dark abyss?
Now strain the eye, arrest the blood's smooth nap. .
Impelling grandeur doth essay to wrap
The Soul of God within this awful curl,

And fill with majesty the springing gap. .
Deep throes and terrors unremitting whirl,
And main and mist alike their gracious gifts unfurl.

And Speech is hushed within its humble home,
Pride is rebuked and poor Self chastened here. .
Behold a world wherein the Soul may roam,
Flying its clay for an exhaustless cheer,
Yet feasting with a reverential fear
And the All-Being's overwhelming board,
Where perfect goodness holds its wide career,
And life is sinewed in the roaring Word
Whose long and loud appeals are felt while they are heard.

And white Earth trembles neath the mighty tread,
Nor dares oppose the monster's headlong way,
Nor mock his groaning voices deep as dread,
Nor parallel his most sublime array. .
For his is a commanding, resolute sway,
That orders homage and obedient love
In the strong thunder of his glory's fray,
And while he wills the sternest will to move
Asserts th' Repose of power that power alone can prove.

Lo, the Skies talk! and Ocean answers back
As each were angered with the other's threat
And would disbattle 'neath his passion's rack. .
And scared Space shudders as two worlds had met.
Each bent to prove itself most passionate,
And hot pursued, pursuing with hot rage,
Outpour the floods of their envenomed debt. .
Grasp! grasp! the story of this fearful page
When Deity and Dust their awful powers engage.

There's, too, a pleasing terror in the sea,
A wild enchantment in its infinite waste,
There is a rapture in its roaring glee,
One language, one, that man has not defaced. .
The lucious land by fertile greenery traced
Has more of nutriment and gentle sweets,
But here where elements by fear are chased
The soul is moved, and shrinks from what it greets,
And roams in reverent awe these curling, liquid streets.

It is enough — here find a sacred height,
A watery Babel where th' spirit may rise
With true ambition to the Source of light. .
But when man lords thee, Sea, and vainly tries
To rule thee, thou dost yield his seeming prize,

Then breakest down the barriers of sense
With thy stern cold negation, and the skies
Of Pride, or mockest at such poor defense,
Rebuking with thy Dreadfulness! Omnipotence!

* * * * * *

Or from this mountain throne the sweeping world!
Beyond, about, ten thousand charms unfurled,
Swell the deep bosom with unfathomed awe,
As sight expounds the 'mensities of law. .
Divinely glad the prospect's wing-ed page,
That ocean, plain and summit doth engage,
A concave floor that joins its roof of glass
To prove great Earth at last all hollowness!

But stay, for though an atom's little part
Of God and Glory here may move thy heart,
Yet let that little entertain and teach,
'Tis all, poor worm, thy present powers may reach. .
In yon expanse that fills the eager gaze
With strange infection and undreamt amaze
Is that which will as well dilate thy thought,
And mark the Teacher in the Lesson taught. .

Magnificently wild the varied scene,
Divided 'twixt deep gray and deeper green,
And the quick sky whose tints exchanged for threats
The round, unruffled ocean wakes and frets;
Now view again immensity's array,
And feel the grandeur of this splendid fray. .

Is there not Passion's self in each strong blast
The Storm-king heralds to yon rocky mast,
To yonder chain of craggy toppling steeps,
And the stern bosom of these troubled deeps?
Lo, the fierce clouds unlock their panting pores
And oceans tumble to their earthy shores,
Conveying life, death, happiness, dismay,
Ere they again shall climb their coming way. .
With voices hoarse that join the sea's loud mirth
In chorus that doth shake the very Earth,
Down the steep sides the springing torrents plunge,
Chill dread succeeding each affrighted lunge;
Breaking at crags that pierce their eager path,
Rock-piles compelling to a yeasty bath,
Filling the gorges and each dark abyss,
Leaping the high o'erhanging precipice,
'Till from the flood and cataract of fear,
The avalanche of waters and despair,

The weeping height is for a season free,
As on they rush to wrestle with the sea.

* * * * * * .

Oh pale, Time-tortured, melancholy hills,
  That with steel-sinewed fortitude hath stood
Against all fires of wrath and wintry chills
      Of child-ingratitude,
Say, will ye further lend your fatherhood
To these new sons and their steel-sinewed wills?
Mayhap your griefs will be less strong than yore,
  This later race perceive your furrowed brows,
Your cheeks, dark-chiseled, where the tear-floods
    tore,
  And learn some sweet compassion for such woes. .
Mayhap though you have wept you'll weep no more,
Else with delight, as when a joy-tide flows
Down your scarred face and gladdens as it goes. .

Or stand a solemn warning of the past,
  A record of the violence of things. .
That e'en the iron world-piles, ribbed and vast,
That stab the heavens, melt in the holocaust
Whose name is Change, and whereunto their clings
Th' eternal seal — *Upharsin* — at the last. .

An awful warning of the doom Decay,
That e'en the bones and props of Earth shall know,
And no thing the Despoiler shall not slay,
Nor any growth that shall not cease to grow,
And yield its atoms to a different day,
Its warm red tides, perchance, to flow a happier way.

Be ye to these the witness of their fate,
And ballast to their equipoise of life ;
Ye clove the cloud-lands once as with a knife,
And all the earth-lands did ye agitate. .
Ah, may these know the privilege of strife,
And timeliness of gifts before too late,
May, these learn from ye Temperance and Peace,
Simplicity and Strength and life's divinest lease.

And gazing on your mighty God-like form,
O masculine mountains ! or when at rest
Or toying with the terrors of the Storm,
And Darkness, when the demon Wrath is guest—
Be moved unto like works of mightiness,
Roused by stern Beauty and Beneficence,
To blessings that magnificently bless ;
Amazed unto devotion and defence ;

Startled from death to most triumphant deeds,
And splendid harvest-hood of Life's sublimest seeds.

Fortitude! Fraternity! these be your song . .
Hear the glad accents leap the lyre along,
A grand, severe, abiding, hardy plea,
That mingles with the thunders of the sea!
Whose patient sufferings scatter from the earth
The pale pretentions of effeminate birth,
As surely warding Luxury's nerveless wand
As sinewed Ocean melts a mount of sand . .
Or Courage! O what strong emotions roll,
Now bound and burn from the enlisted soul!
This is the force God nurtured in your breast
Wherewith to found his Empire of the West,
That men might worship as they best knew how,
And vowing Manhood make their noblest vow.

* * * * * *

Hail! and again! fair Daughter of the West!
Thou jewel of the Ocean, bright and blest,
O, smile ye with thy omnipresent light,
Thine eyes that are a sacrament of sight,
Thy lips that pose an everlasting kiss,
With all thy face and all its freight of bliss . .

For thou art richer in thy beauty's lore,
Than Ocean's self in pearl or precious store,
And lo, thy charms that maketh bitter, sweet,
Inspire the court of nations at thy feet.

How wise was God in making thee so fair,
And curling passion in thy comet hair,
And staining all thy limbs with stain of stars.
That in the warring of thy maiden wars
With th' iron-sinewed tyrannies of Earth,
Thy part, Oh, thine! would be it to give birth
To one more fair and sweet than e'en thyself,
A gladsome, gifted, heaven-conveying elf,
Whose force would be the morning-light of Mind,
Whose work the saviorship of human-kind.

* * * * * *

Sound acclamations! sweep the silver lyre!
And leap, O living Music, to the hour!
Have not been found new strata of desire,
Have not been born new elements of power?
The new day dawn bestows a Glory-shower!
The hallelujahs of the stars are born!
A strong young light pours forth her splendid dower,

Her wild vitality encompassing the morn,
And Hope bounds up and on and yields her harvest-
horn.

O song, O metaphors of praise,
Climb ye and applaud her ways
Till the Sun smiles rapture-smitten, the Stars
Take up and on the vital bars,
Glad'ning the heavens ; 'till the Air
To the everlasting coasts of her,
Be younger for the blissful prayer,
For red Life's unfathomable stir,
The light-haired laughing Clouds a-wing,
Happier for this song to sing . .
Applaud to God's interminable place,
To the world-gamuts of th' almighty heights,
To the vocal, inextinguishable lights —
Till exaltation penetrates all space.

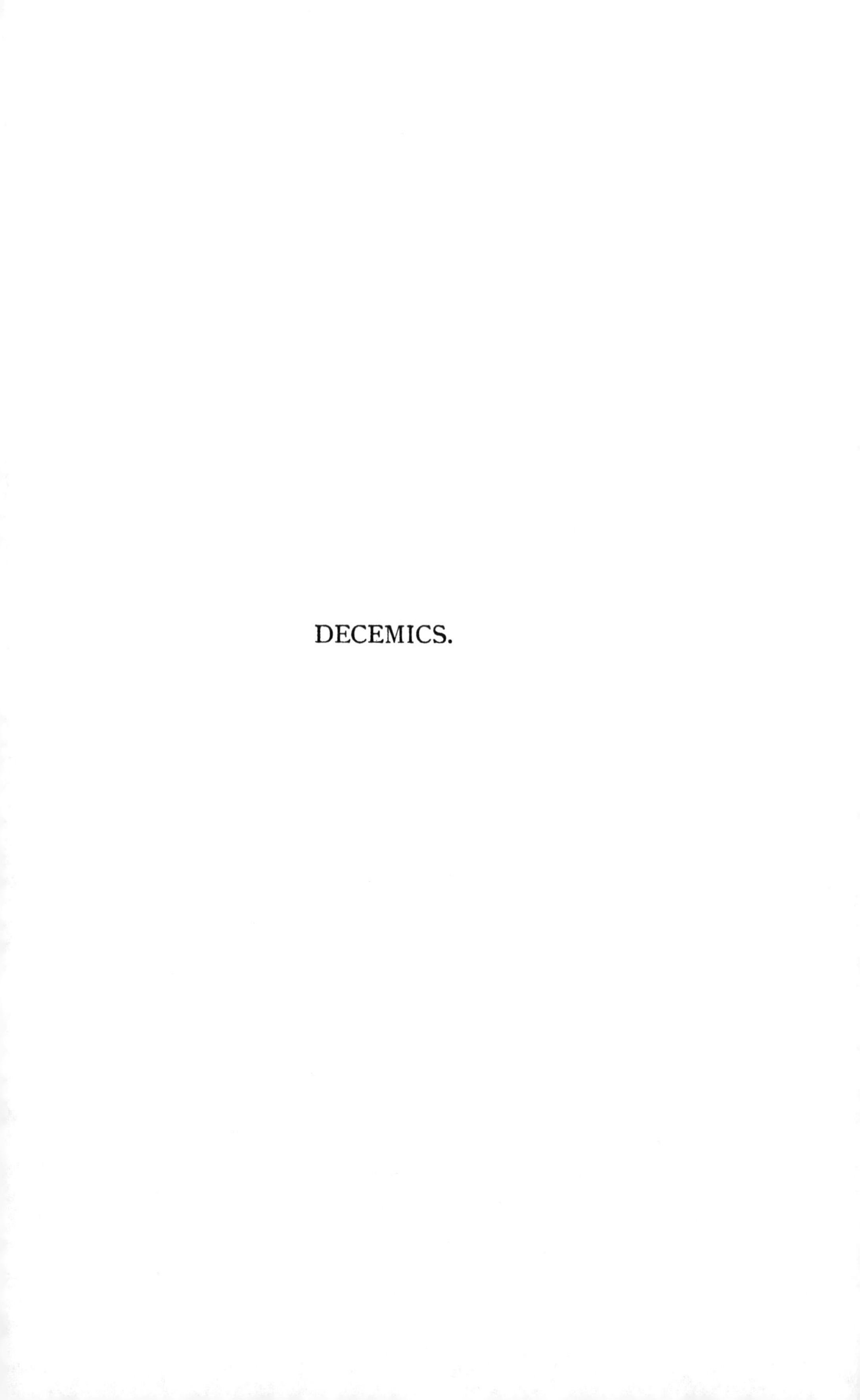

DECEMICS.

I.

WOMAN.

CHASED with fine gold her woman's page appears,
And her rich path with an abundant bliss ;
Deny her not the gentleness she rears,
Praise when aright, forgiveness when amiss,
Else cast her o'er despair's unknown abyss,
Or add fresh fuel to her aching fears :
Blest partner ! nay, she is life's very source ;
Dispensing not alone the nectrous course
To the frail bud she bears, but to the swain,
The hero and the sage with happy force,
Grants a perpetual harvest to sustain,
Life's sweetest stream from an exhaustless vein.

II.

FREEDOM.

THE star-democracy that sprinkles space,
The airy reaches of untutored seas,
The leaping seasons' unconstrain-ed race —
Thou art the breath and sinewy soul of these,
The burden of their myriad harmonies,
Rehearsed in whisper soft or thunder bass :
O, in the rounds of thy untiring flight,
Cleave the cold walk of iron-footed night,
And deeply search the leaden hearts of men,
That they from stars, seas, seasons learn their Right,
Lest drooping, faltering hope expire and then
Exultant chains may mock the might have been.

III.

NIGHT.

INSPIRED Teacher of the gift of Day,
And life's sweet peace, how doth thy coming bless,
And reassure the glory of thy sway ;
Grand is thy presence, but thy strong address
Majestic, woos by its stern tenderness,
And mitigates my else distracted way ;
Here let the pilgrim bare his burning brow,
And hide in thy dear robe the day's last throe,
For thou canst charge with health and hope and teach
With voice divine, forgetfulness of woe ;
Or when mild moons thy wilder forms impeach,
Assert anew how far thy balm may reach.

IV.

BYRON.

A MOUNTAIN torrent with exhaustless source,
Appalling as it hastens to supply,
An Ætnaen flame with undefin-edcourse,
Resplendent in its wild sublimity ;
A power of varied will now low, now high,
Charming and cursing with acutest force,
Far fastening its spell of cunning art,
To gratify, then prey upon the heart ;
O other wonders may unite and blend,
But this was not itself lest wide apart !
Lord of an height none other could transcend,
With its wild loves and will that would not bend.

V.

LINCOLN.

A CHAMPION of humanity and right,
  A man of virtue and of simple thought,
Daring for justice with a deep delight,
  Nor trumpeting what happily he wrought ;
  And day by day an honest duty sought ;
Wielding high charges with unwearied might,
  And by good will won laurels as he rose,
  The stronger love of friends and friends of foes ;
To such belong a place by angels wooed,
  To such a nation her affection owes :
Whose works are seeds that ever are renewed,
Whose lives are battles for the common good.

VI.

TO ERNA.

WHEN Venus 'rose, the issue of a flower,
  Above the silvery mists that veiled the sea,
She wore no charms of a diviner power
  Than thine, sweet Erna, are allowed by me ;
  And my soul sighs an humble prayer to thee —
Most fair enchantress of this midnight hour —
  That with thy smiles thou'lt make my darkness light,
  Create a day to reign where now is night ;
Dispel the forlorn humor of my frame
  With the abundance of thy beauty's might . .
Grant thy sweet seal that I may free my flame,
And lock within my heart thy heart and name.

VII.

TO FESTUS.

THE deep warm summers of a liquid love —
  The leaping beauty of a young glad soul —
The web of life that Love and Beauty wove —
  I pour to thee and thine and drain the bowl !
  Who hast sung the Song and touched the laurel goal,
Who hast won the Bliss when gods have vainly strove.
  Oh, drink who can th' insane lees of life !
  With ecstasy the weapon of the strife . .
Let reason be thy great Love's prisoner,
  And know the sweetness Christ has made thy wife,
The Beautiful that is thy minister —
Thou hast a sure redeemer — it is her !

VIII.

SAPPHO.

ALAS! that Love's lit torch should burn in vain,
That Fate should cut off eloquent desire,
Call forth despair as chorus to thy strain,
And choke with grief where sweet breaths did respire,
Or feed with death lost passion's icy pyre:
Thy lyre and love and lot do yet remain,
The tenth invoked magician of all time!
And the glad muse shall through all æons climb;
Love that was thine ignite, inspire, redeem,
Song that was thine make beauty more sublime. .
Ah, destiny that named thy life a dream
Has mocked herself and given the world a theme.

ODES.

Ode I.

"FINE WAS HIS VOICE."

FINE was his voice whose ruddy lip
The Hebla bees once sought to sip,
And sweet the tone
The siren wings from her fatal throne. .
But finer far the finished tongue,
And sweeter far the silver lung
Which drops *her* pregnant name. .
Which holds fierce mem'ries in serene control,
And echoes gladness to my deepest soul —
"*Minne!*"
The Beauty-flame —
Which tells that pregnant name.

Fast to the voice's wing
A thousand graces cling
All, all her own ;
They come and bless and linger one by one,

Inspiring gracious praises all her own,
And go and come,
To leave a bloom upon the inmost heart,
An halcyon delight,
A joy her beauty-being doth impart,
With soft entrancing might,
And while unmindful of all else beside,
It renders smooth the breast of pleasure's tide.

And thus it sings,
That inner tongue, and here the tale it brings—

"Fair! fair!
To Beauty's despair,
As she were born in the womb of the rose,
And nursed by the snows. .
The light of the skies is dyed in her hair—
Fair! fair!

"Sweet! Sweet!
From face unto feet,
Her tinted charms are mistaken for flowers;
Like myrrh are her hours. .
Her blisses more keen than nectar of wheat—
Sweet! sweet!

And it fills with rapture the moment's space
With a theme as bright as a comet's face —
None fitter to rejoice —
And the beautiful line of her life I trace
By advices from the voice,
Which holds quick mem'ries in serene control,
And echoes gladness to my deepest soul —
"Minne!"
The beauty-flame —
Which tells that pregnant name.

Ode II.

PAY FOR YOUR LIFE AS YOU LIVE IT.

WOULD ye be master of what ye are,
The lord of your own dear life?
Away with the reed
That will cause you to bleed,
For behold! 'tis a two-edged knife!
And lo! your wounds are as deep as night,
Your chains tear your flesh with their tyrant might,
You're a slave! ah, a slave!
In a breathing grave,
With hope from nor friend nor flight.

O pay for your life as you live it!
Now furl it in signs of gold;
If you would be free
Heed this prayer and plea,
Nor be wrung in the serpent's fold;

His smiles are as false as his face is fair,
His promises empty and fleeting as air,
        And all will forsake
        At the captive stake,
    Then away from the fatal snare.

Fall if you will in some cause of good,
    On some glorious field of strife,
        Die! die! in your tracks,
        But O not in the racks
    Of a languishing, dying life:
Let your arm be loosed and your heart be light,
'Till your parting breath's unfettered flight,
        Nor perish a slave
        In a breathing grave,
    And the toils of a barren night.

Ode III.

BREAK! BREAK! O SOUL!

BREAK! break O soul! from the bonds of clay,
 Away with the speed of light,
Away for a space to a higher day
 With an exultant flight,
And bless upon thy eager way,
 Thy resurrection's might.

Is earth too small for thee, great heart?
 Then speed on thy airy wing;
Else were thy earth a subtle smart
 All thy peace poisoning,
That thou dost yearn for another part,
 A life that knows no sting?

Nay, nay, arise with thy wild ideal
 And scan each world of space;
Thou wilt not know thy picture real

When is closed thy foolish chase,
But happier be to know and feel
Thy heaven no idle place.

No dreamland vain with its idle life,
Nor realm of covetous bliss,
But a place of God-inspir-ed strife,
That undevelopment's abyss
Shall with the fruits of growth be rife ;
Say, is not heaven in this?

Ode IV.

APART FROM LOVE.

MY heart was a spirit replete with peace,
    Because of a love it knew,
But fate commanded a sore release
    From this worship intense and true,
And the joy of my spirit-heart was flown,
'Twas cursed and cold, 'twas heavy and lone,
    And its very bliss did rue.

My soul was a sun of burning flame,
    With seeming immortal rays,
Which triumphed and smiled over night and shame,
    Over night and night-like days ;
But at once 'twas dark where this heaven shone,
Its warm rich gold was eclipsed and gone,
    And earth was a tangled maze.

My life was a stream of still pure blood,
Where passion-flowers did grow;
Silent and smooth the deepening flood,
Even and ever its flow;
Yet lo! its current was damned anon,
'Till its stayed tears every stay o'errun,
Its sea of love to show.

ODE V.

O WHERE ARE MY TREASURES?

O WHERE are my treasures,
My joys and my pleasures?

. . . . . .

Call Death, foolish heart, now call thou his name,
If he *is*, and hath reaped them, he'll give thee the same.

O where are my flowers that bloomed in the morning,
In spring-time, O yes, in their spring-time and mine!
Ah me! have they gone with their bright blooming morning,
Gone from their shrine?

O where are my birds that sang in the morning,
In spring-time, O yes, in their spring-time and mine?
Alas! have they flown with their rich ringing morning,
My feathery nine?

O where are my suns that shone in the morning,
In spring-time, O yes, in their spring-time and mine!

O say ! have they sunk with their glad golden morning,
No more to shine ?

O where all my joys that lived in the morning,
In spring-time, O yes in their spring-time and mine !
Now speak, have they died with their new natal morning,
While here I repine ?

But no answer came,
For Death had no claim,
Had he *been* and had reaped them,
He had given the same.

Yet a change came a day,
Turning night into day,
And thus sang the heart
On its happier way :

Ah ! now I am back with my Spring's early hours,
With my treasures, my suns, my birds and my flowers,
Their morning and mine shall be mine still forever ;
'Twas the passage of earth only seeming to sever
My heart and its jewels and joys.

Ode VI.

THY NAKED FEET.

SITTING by thy naked feet,
Farinella, lovely thing,
Magical emotions spring,
Filling th' fonts of life replete—
Sitting by thy feet.

Worshiping two marble feet,
Streaked with tiny truant veins,
Purple, pretty, precious stains,
Let time be less cruel fleet—
Worshiping thy feet.

Loving slight and tender feet,
Carved like ivory keys to thrill,
Brain and breast alike they fill,
Heart of hearts with raptures beat—
Loving tender feet.

Petting pink and lily feet,
  Soft and warm and closely pressed,
  Deep their lover's dear unrest,
White round ankles peep and greet —
    Petting lily feet.

Caressing both thy velvet feet
  Drinking blisses warm with sighs,
  Bound beneath seducing eyes,
Love! prolong this heaven sweet —
    Caressing velvet feet.

Ode VII.

THE CHANGES OF THE SHELL.

WHILOM I struck the changes of my shell,
The soul strings of a varied instrument,
To me and to all willing list'ners lent —
And gathered thus the accents as they fell.

FIRST CHANGE.

Responsible, immortal Choice,
One with the Disposer, Will,
Choice that is poor Self-hood's voice,
Will whose tongue cannot be still,
Joyous that it *can* rejoice —
O privilege of weal or woe,
O Freedom born with birth of life,
O death to die, O growth to grow,
Desire that is the darling strife. . .
Let men pursue the loves and hates,
The pains and pleasures as they fly,

The truths and lies that Time relates,
  And dare the boasts of destiny.

SECOND CHANGE.

The wake that traverses the dark,
  And hisses through the sullen gloom —
    Dark that hath no single spark,
    Gloom whose kinship is the tomb,
    And no thing to prove an ark —
Now shall the passage be of light,
  Now Understanding lead the way,
One thing can cleave the mask of night,
  And bid its barrenness be day,
Convert sweet Peace to be a guest,
  Give Pain the summons to depart,
Show weariness the place of rest,
  And happiness the troubled heart.

THIRD CHANGE.

The Truth of one that is a Lie
  When issued from another's brain —
    Lie because it did not cry
    "Train me to a riper strain,
    Teach me to arise and fly . ."

That thing which is a growth replete,
 The stature of a word or deed,
The sweetness of a life when sweet,
 The blood that's given it to bleed,
The Whole that cannot beg nor lend,
 Ripened fruit of earth and space,
Perfection of an act or end,
 And very head-light of the race.

FOURTH CHANGE.

Virtue — that is the child of Truth,
 And of whom Wisdom is the sire —
  Truth that is perennial youth,
  Fire that is not made of ire,
  That slays the canker and the tooth -
O Strength where weakness would have been
 O Health where lean decay had clung,
Teach aspiration how to win,
 And youth the cunning to be young,
Discover with thy sober charm
 The triumphs of the passing hour,
That Vigilance which conquers harm,
 That Temperance whose name is Power.

FIFTH CHANGE.

Th' divine Form and Grace of things,
And th' quick soul of grace and form —
Things to which completion clings,
Form O stronger than the storm,
Nature's happier offerings —
God saw the reason for this same,
The proud warm argument of life,
The inspiration without name,
The Beauty man would take to wife,
And lo, it fills the earth and air,
O sweetness to repletion grown,
O Woman fairer than aught fair,
O all that's charmful to be known.

SIXTH CHANGE.

The Love that is the Soul of all,
And crowning victory of God!
ll — replete as is a ball —
God because outgrown the rod,
Glory that outlives the gall —
O this is that fair Queen of Kings,
That so well marries heart to heart,

The vital web that weds all things,
  And makes them forget to part,
The fullest answer to all prayer,
  The precious universal leaven,
Reward of ev'ry cross we bear,
  And Substance of immortal Heaven.

Ode VIII.

"STAND LIKE AN ANVIL."*

O BURY the hatchet — 'tis done, brothers, done,
We will still be the chain freedom wrought us ;
Let the last worthy son
Of the great Washington,
Hail the stars that our father has bought us :
O let us be kindred in heart as in birth,
Let fratenal love tell American worth,
To-day, to-morrow — forever ;
Let us join heart and hand,
Like a pyramid stand,
Like a ship breasting every weather,
Let us stand, brothers, stand,
For our free common land,
Let us stand like an anvil together.

*"Stand like an anvil," The message from Ignacius Theophorus to Polycarp.

O, pass the peace-pipe, — pass it on — pass it on —
'Till the last brother freeman shall hail it !
'Till the last worthy son
Of the good Washington,
Shall forget his last thought to assail it ;
O, let us be firm in the cause of our soil,
Our hearths and our hearts were not forged for a spoil,
Nor warmed with the instinct to sever !
Let us join heart and hand,
Like a monument stand,
Like a rock breasting every weather,
Let us stand, brothers, stand,
For our free common land,
Let us stand like an anvil together.

Ode IX.

"I SAW THEE AND I LOVED THEE."

I SAW thee and I loved thee!
  But 'twere vain to chase the cunning
Of the mystery that moved me . .

. . .

For the thousand springs that gladdened,
The ten thousand stings that maddened,
  Stayed and held my captured being,
O were subtler than could ever,
  Ever yield to simple seeing:
All my deep soul's deepest knowing
  Felt and blessed the ministrations,
Knew thy soul's sublime o'erflowing,
  Keenly felt its inspirations,
Each profound and pure bestowing,
  With affection's best endeavor,
  And the blessing of a lover.

I saw thee and I loved thee!
  But I cannot tell the secret
Of the mightiness that moved me. .

. . .

For Love in thy tresses nestled,
  Touched the rose-hue of thy cheek,
With thy winning habits wrestled,
  Thy glad habits that could speak,
Love provoked thy tongue's persuasions,
  Lit the torches of thine eyes,
Moved thy touches' ministrations,
  And thy motions' melodies,
And the atmosphere about thee,
Had been loveless if without thee,
  And the magnet so imbedded
  In the presence I had wedded,
Drew me with a power to thee,
'Till my deepest soul did woo thee.

I saw thee and I loved thee!
  But 'twere vain to seek the meaning
Of the ministry that moved me.

Ode X.

FRANCE.

(Written during the Franco-Prussian War.)

I.

AFAR, and high and low, among the strong,
  O dreadful tribulation, dread as death,
And weeping amid strength and breath of wrong,
  Tears which incite a bold and mighty breath,
Weepings that nerve and groanings that make great,
O stern lamentings of a travailed world,
          O carnage of hate,
          Death-lust insatiate,
How hath Revenge upon Hope madly hurled?
How devastating hath her blood-flames curled?
          How in the night
          Hath the sword of might,
Pierced the proud Soul and drank her light!

Cleaving all bare her virgin wealth of grace,
And subtle lovliness, and snapped the right,
And gave rejoicings o'er her dire disgrace,
As there were day-stars in her vacant sight,
As there were summers in her empty place.

II.

Let wave on wave e'er shake the rock foundations,
Oceans appall and drown, and deserts lose,
King Time exhaust his deadliest ministrations,
Obedient flame and sword their last spark use,
What then, O thou great Equaler of stations,
Freedom, dear life — who blesses where she sues —
Wilt cease thy melting, moulding inspirations,
Thy hope relinquish and thy heaven refuse?
Will thy deep soul forget its deep durations,
Thy hand its health, thy voice the God it woos?
Nay! thy live sparks — eternal constellations —
Shall o'er the tomb of Time their triumph muse,
And vain, forever vain, Hate's imputations,
Fetters and wars, which thy sweet breath accuse,
O grand thy throes and self-imposed privations,
For thou'lt surmount the sod thy blood imbrues,
And thine immortal spirit's emanations
Fill with resplendent light where light alone subdues.

III.

O Life death driven,
O Death life given,
O Morn night riven,
When shall the Day appear?
Time of fraternity,
End of infirmity,
Justice eternally!
Tell us how near;
Mercy's maternity
O hasten here.

IV.

Hasten, for lo! all is cold, deaf and dark;
The hour is beneath its loud vaunted acclaim,
On the tide of red carnage bear Liberty's ark,
Come! tell thou the hour of its lie and its shame;
And fill earth and sky
With thy glad ministry,
O teach now the way to thy God-planted mark,
Thy beauty of force and blessing of flame.

V.

But a Voice is abroad —
The teacher of day with a thousand true tongues.
With the flow'ret's breath and the cannon's loud lungs,
With a sound that is awed,
And whose varied vein,
With an infinite youth and immortal strain
Doth the soul-world quicken by feld and flood —
Is abroad with shame for the rule of blood,
And the empire of pain.

VI.

O time-mocking France, O pregnant with fire,
Swell still the wide chorus of day to the powers,
And higher and higher,
Re-echo the chorus of day to the hours.

VII.

Deep is the boast of valor 'mong the nations,
The pride of prowess and titanic thews ;
False is the sword and valor's desolations,
The wild onsettings which forlorn hope rues ;
O how ripe Truth doth mourn her desecrations,
So Courage, France, hath crowned thee to abuse ;

O tear the page from thy new generations,
  Let thy voice glad the day thy Truth renews,
Then shall the skies console thy lamentations,
  The might of Justice thy name's might infuse,
Then shall Life sound her leaping acclamations,
  And light and love submit the genius of their hues.

VIII.

Come, then, eternal progress, muse her praise!
  Come, re-baptise her with a splendid hope!
Crown her with soul and sinew quick'ning bays,
  Arm her with rich triumph's richest scope.

IX.

Scarred in thy grand defense,
Teacher of excellence,
Rise in thy ashes red and sackcloth of thy woe,
O thou so trebly wronged,
O thou immortal tongued,
How canst thou err in bidding thy great life to flow?
If thy proud nature err'd,
Virtue hath error stirred,
For out of guilty bars and darkness thou hast leaped;
Others have miss'd the right,
Aiming at lesser light

Than has inspired thy soul and thy glad sinews steeped;
O not while there remains
One life-spark in thy veins,
Cease to assert and claim the kingdom of thy place;
Hold to this life to thee,
God-given Liberty!
Drown with thy tears and blood conscription's latest trace;
Wash thy robes new and white,
Cleanse the last stain of night,
Climb with the wings of fire and fervor of the wind,
And may thy peerless plan,
Soul-stirred Republican!
Fill high thy burning hope and empire of thy mind.

MISCELLANEOUS.

GOD SPEED TO MEN.

SPEED ye, God speed, upon the race of life,
To all men speed and gracious stars and song,
The strife of good — let that become the strife,
And all forget one thing — forget to wrong.

Alas, there is enough that needs must be
To mock at hope and cross our anxious way,
Let no hand then afflict the prostrate knee,
No wanton shadow fill the room of day.

'Twere better to raise up this troubled thing,
And brush some burden from her onward path,
To cheer a soul is easy as to wring,
And tender courage stronger is than wrath.

Bid him God speed, the struggling child of pain,
By wrong or error or misfortune won,
He needs no more cold links upon his chain,
Nor added gauntlets of despair to run.

He is most man who blesses as he goes,
  Most woman — who inspires divinest deeds,
That circumscribes the awful waste of woes,
  That heals — as woman can — the soul that bleeds.

Peace, peace on earth, good will, God speed to men,
  All hail and triumph now and to the end,
The endless end when Hope is won and when
  Great man finds man the universal friend.

MY LOVE'S THE LIFE.

SHE is brightness to my day-time,
  A star-sun to my night,
My constant, precious ray-time,
  The all I know of light;
My love's the life of color, too,
  Fair Nature's painted tide,
My love's the life of every hue,
  My love is more beside.

O Music, fill thou all my soul —
  My love is in each strain —
Thy rich, red languishings shall roll
  Throughout my breast and brain,
And raise me with a glad rebound —
  O warm, O liquid bride —
My love's the life of burning sound,
  My love is more beside.

Ah, sweetness of the flower-cups,
  And drippings of the vine,
The burden that the bee sups
  Is of this sweet of mine,
Ah, rapture where the lip clings,
  Ripe fruitage deified,
My love's the life of honeyed things,
  My love is more beside.

The odor of the wildwood,
  And perfume of the grove,
Were caught up with her childhood,
  And nurtured with my love,
Ah, brightness, beauty, sweet distress,
  Delights 'till now denied,
My love's the life of blissfulness,
  My love is more beside.

"LET US BE CONSCIOUS HOW HAPPY WE ARE."

LET us be conscious how happy we are,
  That the summer of life is our own,
The winter that stings and the shadows that mar,
  Have warmed in the stars that have shone;
Our years are as acts of a joyous dream,
  Our moments as rays of a sun,
Our lives are the flood of a master stream,
  Two streams that have mingled in one.

Let us be conscious how happy we are,
  For contentment has sweetened our earth;
To the crowd we resign the discords that jar,
  To the desert surrender its dearth;
We have learned to fathom the deeps of our day,
  Have caught the fine music of things,
We have courted the burden of sweets on our way,
  But conquered its burden of stings.

"O PEACE! SWEET PEACE!"

O PEACE! sweet Peace! how glad thy temperate reigns,
By thee is joy — with thee alone remains;
Thy hand alone canst hail and stay the horn,
And golden sunburst of perpetual morn:

. . .

The seas are clean — no fierce Armada's sail,
Is urged to conquest by the guiltless gale,
No armament yon swelling bosom strews
With threats of blood to stain its native hues,
And the proud land from coast to happy coast
Asks not which part doth love, but which loves most.

It is a time for gratitude and praise,
An hallowed harvest of enriching days,
Where strength unmaimed asserts its proper might,
And blessed health assures the reign of right;
No private gain the public good assails,

Beneath the shade of Law's impartial scales,
Nor helpless virtue weeping for a friend,
Contracts the promise of a woful end;
Teems far and near the fruits of honest toil,
Full garners speak the well attended soil,
And tasteful wealth the finer arts sustain,
The painter's story and the poet's strain.

And War is weakness by thy sinewed sway;
Aye! thou art stronger than an ocean fray
When wildest tempests plow their watery path,
'Till sea on sea augments the common wrath;
Yet when War's tread, or Discord's noisy tongue,
Resound their threats to do old Time a wrong,
Thy virtue's strength quick veils the rising feud,
And bars thy presence from the serpent brood.

URLINE.

WE parted some dead days ago, Urline,
Yet do you haunt me like a spectral rhyme ;
I feel your presence though apart, unseen,
As in our sunny passion's morning-time.

When the strange tints of love-flowers cut like wine,
Marking our life-beats by their sharpened blow,
When fires that burn compressed your years and mine
To th' insane glory of a moment's throe.

Ah, I do feel you with me just as then,
Not all the same, and yet so like of yore,
That I am thrilled to gladness and to pain,
Acutest pain and gladness as before.

All through the love-lit labyrinths of my life
The naked touches of your warm white breath
Have stung like cleavings of a whetted knife
And palpitations of a dream-land death.

We said adieu cold years ago, Urline,
  With words alone. . how apt was each sick heart
To stay the tortures of that last lorn scene —
  Say, will our souls e'er speak farewell and part?

For our dear loving, gentle, was a dream,
  A palace of rich chambers raised to fall,
A promise vainly cast upon life's stream,
  A fierce deep draught of nectar and of gall.

"CALL NOT THE PROMISE VAIN."

CALL not the promise vain, Camille,
  Call not the prospect dark;
Have we not wealth in rosy health,
  And youth for a sturdy bark?
Is the world not wide with ready work
  For ready hands to do,
And will not my heart play an earnest part
  When invoked by love and you?

Call not the promise vain, Camille,
  Call not the prospect dark,
Is their not life in very strife
  When happiness — the mark?
Is there not strength in the depth and hight
  Of bliss we hold in view,
And will not my heart play a stubborn part
  When inspired by love and you?

Call not the promise vain, Camille,
  Call not the prospect dark,
Let courage bold our lives enfold,
  And labor be our ark ;
Is there not cheer in our path of hope,
  Will not success pursue,
And will not my heart play a manly part
  When inflamed by love and you ?

"COME!"

ABOVE all sounds of the eloquent earth
A cry smote my ear
Like a rose's cry as it springs to birth,
One slight wild word, but a heaven of cheer,
A lisp that conveyed all the songs of a year –
"Come!"

To that which in one is your white, red and blue,
All below, all above,
To the Augusta and Lucia of you,
To the bosom all burdens of balm are of,
To her your embrace and your soul of love —
"Come!"

If joy be sought by your staggering feet,
Or bliss be your quest,
If you yearn to discover the sweets that are sweet,
If eager to find out the way that is best,
If weary in search of the jewel of rest —
"Come!"

THE MINISTRY OF NATURE.

A FRAGMENT.

I.

WHEN in the race of life or care or pain
Weigh heavily upon you or the blight
Of disappointed hope ; when come again
Vague forms of dearer days shedding the light
Of ghostly-seeming bliss, list to a strain
From Nature as her happy haunts invite
Sincere communion, and attempt to feel
The peace, the joy that she will then reveal.

II.

Go forth alone, confiding, and make her
Your priest ; confess, resolve, amend ; there find
What you should have, a worthy minister,
And forms for every taste ; have but a mind
To do and be advised ; do not incur
A needless censure, but contrive to bind
In one triumphant whole, apart from strife,
The being, aim and end of earthly life.

III.

There find society without a sting,
There learn a language of the sweetest tone,
There view the beautiful — a perfect thing,
There feel companionship with God alone,
There hear the melody that angels bring,
There know the glory that alone is known
In atmospheres of unity and love,
And 'mid the powers that melt and mould and move.

IV.

Seek one of those bright-painted balmy eves
That have a vital freshness for the heart;
One that a day of storm so often leaves,
When Sol's emblazoned blushes slowly part
Their deep'ning hues from eyes their absence grieves;
When flirting fires like angel beacons start,
Weaving their scarlet hair with ermine shrouds,
And with strange gold embroidering the clouds.

V.

There's then a glory in the trackless wood
That passes rivalry; a sense that in
Its first and highest sympathy with good,
Inspires profoundest awe; far from the din

Of marts in sacred isolation, why should
There not exist a presence half divine,
That may be wooed and won — and that instills
A fire celestial in the soul it fills.

VI.

The moon arises and her lucious beams,
Soft, warm and feminine, steal gently
O'er the hills . . a dream of light ; the earth seems
Filled with heaven's atmosphere ; the sentry
Stars with eyes of gold look down on streams,
And vales and fields of sheen, marking intently
How all sweet Life bestows her varied bliss,
Or Beauty pouts her universal kiss.

VII.

O woodland wild ! thou hast a pleasure dear
As life ; a something passionately loved
Ever pervades thy throbbing grandeur here
In these far depths of solemn shade unroved ;
There is an inspiration in thy cheer
That leaves alone the bristling throng unmoved,
A ratifying grace and bounty given,
That draws the soul to virtue and to heaven.

. . .

VIII.

But lo! the monarch-mountains! from their thrones
That boldly pierce the jeweled vaults of blue,
To the lulled lake below, there echo tones
Of music and of strength; 'tis not for you
Nor me to know them half, yet their rock-bones
Have converse and an eloquence most true
And rapturous born with their birth of fire:
Pause ye and list to Nature's magic lyre!

IX.

Ambitiously they raise their tall heads to
The sky and stand in majesty; broken
And wild and vast and steep and stern but true
To strictest order; e'en their frowns betoken
Excellence, and forest-robed or nude, new,
Old, convulsed or calm, they have unspoken
Joy that waits communion, and a glee,
That fain would plead 'twere bliss enough — to be.

X.

Unto thy mighty and commanding hights,
Thou dome of rocks and monument of power,
Let me my tribute bring; thy mien excites
Profoundest reverence; not thine to cower,

Nor yield thy strength nor yoke thy manhood's
rights,
Nor feel a shudder for the direst hour ;
But like a world's guardian thou dost stand,
Force in the face and fear within thy hand.

* * * * *

XI.

Convert us to thee, Nature ! thy kind forms
Teach more impressively than words of men
The all benificence and bliss ; bright morn's
Refreshing gifts ; its living breeze to fan
The sweet perfumes ; the evening's glow that warms
Us into rapture ; the sky's clear deep span ;
Night's mellow majesty and th' green glad sea,
Conspire to fill our souls with love and thee.

XII.

How full, how fond, how free, how fresh, how fair,
How passing lovely how supremely grand,
How grave and yet how gay, how more than rare,
How wonderful His works. Entranced you stand
And glorify, adore, exult ; a prayer
Of gratefulness your offering poor, and
The deeply pure affection of a soul
That scans with awe creation's boundless scroll.

"ON! EVER ON!"

ON, ever on, with a sturdy devotion,
  A will stout and strong as the wind of the sea,
A purpose as fixed as the rocks of old ocean,
  A heart brave as his heart who dares to be free:
      O on! sternly on!

On, youth, nor be stayed by the toils of temptation,
  One moment has vanquished great kingdoms and
    souls;
On, maiden, nor pause in thy path's elevation,
  Nor risk thy rich bark upon perilous shoals:
      But on! straightly on!

Push on! nobly on! in thy course wisely taken,
  There's pleasure and health in a duty well done,
With Faith rooted deep and with Courage unshaken,
  Sweet Peace will reward a true race truly run:
      Then on! surely on!

Strive on! toiler, on! all nature is moving,
  And alive to the task which her God has imposed;
Be on! human, on! thy proud mastery proving,
  True to the light which to Mind is disclosed:
    O on! stoutly on!

THE KISS.

I KISSED her! the image that Love chose of Life,
To be the white mark of a hallow-ed strife,
And drawn by glad force to her presence of fire,
Learned the story of joy through a spark of desire;
No language of vocal pretentions can tell
The glorious thrill of that magical spell,
'Twas only the sweet pantomime of a kiss,
Could prove my devotion and measure my bliss.

I kissed her! 'twere almost a sin to unfold
From the fervor so fond of that passionate hold,
When all toils of life and all terrors of death
Succumbed to the charm of her soft-sighing breath,
That quickened the soul with delicious unrest,
Warm breast pillowed low upon quivering breast,
Each lip answering back the ripe lip that it greets,
Ever bruised ever yielding its vintage of sweets.

I kissed her! no greater delight could I seek
Than communion so close with that eloquent cheek,
Where the rose tint of youth, passion's beautiful flush,
Tells the heart's burning love by its kindling blush,
While a lustre as bright as e'er beamed from on high
Streamed roguishly forth from a soul-stirring eye,
While the waking of soul, leaping ecstasy's birth,
Asserted the empire of heaven on earth.

"TO WED, OR NOT TO WED?"

(PARAPHRASE.)

TO wed or not to wed, that is the question —
Whether 'tis nicer in the Bach to suffer
The smiles and banters of bewitching females,
Or reach forth arms toward a seige of troubles,
And, by embracing, end them? To woo, to wed,
No more a Bach; and by a wedding say we end
The heart-ache, and the thousand forlornnesses
That men are heir to — 'tis a consummation
Devoutly to be wished. To woo, — to wed; —
To wed! perchance to rue; ah, there's the rub!
For in that fix what after-thoughts may come,
When we have shuffled off our bachelorhood,
Must give us pause: there's the respect,
That makes men live so long a single life;
For who would bear the witcheries of our girls,
The hints of widows, the jokes of ancient maids,
The stern exclusiveness of wintry nights,

Of undarned socks and shirts all buttonless,
When he himself might his quintessence make
With — *Madam, will you assume the responsibitity, etc.*, ?
Who would, fair belles, swear and suffer under such a
life,
But that the dread of something after marriage –
The undesected yoking from whose knots
No bachelor returns — puzzles the will,
And makes us rather bear the ills we have
Than fly to others — when forthcoming results
are in embarrassing unknowableness.

"THROUGH THE RAYS SERENE."

ON AN INFANT'S DEATH.

THROUGH the rays serene of a morning sun,
By heaven blessed and by beauty won,
A tiny dewdrop fell;
In an acorn cup a retreat it found,
And the moments sped in a gentle round
Above the sparkling cell.

But twilight followed the sinking sun,
And night pursued — its day was done —
Short was its earth-life breath;
A Frost approached with a stealthy bound,
And about the gem his cold arm wound,
And the change was counted — Death.

"BUT IF THE HIGH ESTATE OF LOVE SHOULD FAIL?"

BUT if the high estate of Love should fail,
And cast my bankrupt soul back on herself,
Torn and fragmented unto hell's despair —
O what can I to heal my being then?

Quick woo her in some other of her forms . .
If Love shall wound let Love be thy Physician;
If Love kill thee let Love restore thy life;
Oh, hold it a forlorn philosophy
That yields to a despair — take up thy peace
And bear it in the vice of thy brave hand!
Say to the love that measures thee despite —
'Now will I woo thy fair twin-sister's face,
Search out her jailor witcheries, like thine;
Her lips, sweet, like thy lips; her poison breath
That burns as thy breath burns, melting my life;
Her scented hair that wraps about me close;
Her haughty breasts, like thine, silken as snow,

With their contagious pulses of delight ;
Her hard encirclings like a white snake's folds. .
The soul's asylum from its wildest woe.

Thus when by Love's rejection thou hast sought
This kindred form to fill thy being up,
The beauteous flame that flirted with thy life
Will be the only loser of ye twain,
Catching of wisdom at the empty roots
Where thou art climbing with the wings of bliss.

POESY.

SWEET Poesy! thy gracious gifts to me
Do come so heavenly-freighted and refined,
So laden with enchanting mystery,
Crowned with delights the kindest of the kind,
And all awaking ecstasy of mind,
That I embrace thee with a frantic zeal,
Letting each wound of life thy rich balm find,
Or when distractions o'er my bosom steal,
Turn to thy nectrous spring and not in vain appeal.

TO A FEATHER!

HAIL! thou light aerial attribute
Of some ambitious biped of creation;
Who dares to say that thou art destitute
Of fame, crowns, dignities and station?
Indeed thou hast just reasons to be proud,
For many are thy praises, and those loud.

Various are thy callings and thy uses,
As various as thy colors and thy size;
Thy virtue firm, but various thy abuses,
And various the stories thence arise;
Now 'tis a shame the way thou'rt sometimes treated,
But we all know it is not justly meted.

The world at large — and know that it is said
That thou art patronized by all the world —
Makes use of thee when it absconds to bed
Most lackey-like — this is not hurled
At thee as insult, for all the land will vouch
Thy most exhaustless merit in a couch.

Lo! the poor Indian, in his streak-ed state,
(Tho' we admit it is a silly prank,)
Paints thee from fancy at a horrid rate
To symbolize his victories and rank;
Then whiter Indians whiter wills unsheath,
And put thee on the war-path of their teeth.

Yet still the tactic warriors claim their right
To strut thee in thy glory and thy bloom,
Thou has been borne through many a bloody fight
Amid which shone the chieftain's haughty plume;
And then a knight thyself hast been in war,
'Twas thee who led the army of Navarre.

In all these stations thou hast done thy part,
Done well, and all do give thee honor;
Yet more than these thou'st link'd thyself with art
And prov'd thyself a most free-hearted donor;
Thou'st been transformed into an awful pen
To be the slave of literary men.

A slave ! but ah ! a indeed, a glorious one ;
An instrument of destiny and fate ;
Thy cause is known as a laborious one,
And fraught with frauds astounding to relate ;
A tyrant-slave, by whose mysterious power
Saints are set up and up-set in an hour.

Thou'st writ the lives of lions and of kings
Beginning back as far as Father Midden,
Knights, prodigies and gods and other things,
And flaunted what they did and what they
did n't ;
Tis said that thou art mightier than the sword :
All hail thee then, a conqueror and a lord !

MIGNON.

BRIGHT are the crystal stars and gay,
O, bright the diamond's vital ray,
The lakelet bright 'neath a silvery moon,
Brighter than these or the sheen of noon,
Are the eyes of dear Mignon.

Sweet is the virgin breath of Spring,
Sweet th' burdens the bee doth bring,
Sweet is the cup of the honeyed flower,
Sweeter than either in living power,
Are the lips of my Mignon.

Soft are the folds of the snowy rose,
The mossy bed whereon dews repose,
Soft the white plumage of the swan,
Softer and whiter than finest down,
Is the breast of pure Mignon.

Fine are the hymns in the leafy vale,
Rich are the tones of the nightingale,
Dear is the song of the rippling rill,
But finer and richer and dearer still,
Is the voice of sweet Mignon.

Pure is the blossom and bud new born,
Pure the luculent beads of morn,
The lily pure and feathery foam,
But purer still in its happy home,
Is the heart of loved Mignon.

THE FINDING OF YOLONDE.

I HAVE found Yolonde with the yellow hair. .
Her — the ideal of poet-lovers —
The fine foam-dream made into fact,
The second from the womb whence Helen sprung
To madden and exalt the older day.

Ah, the close chase for this reality,
Outdistancing all phantom-idoltry,
And unsubstantial prophecies of hope ;
Now, Love-illumed, provoke your luscious works,
O thou ! the conflagration of the soul !
Or beauty-dawn, star-browed and fair,
Forth broke from the embraces of the Night.

And it were hard for more of joy to be. .
What of th' scented airs of Idumæa,
And the charm-songs of the sirens ?
To me she is the burden of all sweets,
With exhalations of the youthful morn,
And music soft as Lydias'.

Suffer me right near to you, Yolonde,
For distance is despair. .
To quit you, then, were one thing more—despair !
Your being hath a potent witchery
I know to overwhelming,
And in my passion-faith believe it good. .
There are strange odorous stings about you,
Caught mayhap from incense-atmospheres,
The perfume-worship of the goddesses. .
And they steal forth with every move of you ;
Beneath your pregnant touches ;
The drapery that hides your awful riches ;
Your hair. . ah, from your hair Yolonde. .
What young glad suns lent you their gold
To stain it ? the crown
Whose silken sceptre sways by Beauty's force,
Cast forth in grace like circling comet-light.

But how in this same yellow hair, Yolonde,
Shall I find rest and calm of life ?
I may lie in it drunken,
And helpless beneath your fascination. .
Alas ! there were such peril then,
Lest on your breasts —

Falling in a charmed surrender—
My life shall hold its breath, and go!
  Ceasing to be—for ecstasy.

Or in the vibrations of strange chords,
  The inner temple's muse,
Sweet as the love-lisps of angelic tongues,
  Whence my white captor have you come,
  Whither dost lead me with your sorcery,
  And wherefore to my proud repletion?
Am I not full enough of you,
Having you at my soul's anchorage,
  And where my spirit fastens to its God?

Well, you are and must be, th' interpreter,
  Of all of this deep mystery;
Illumining my labyrinthine way,
Crossed and up-ploughed by dragon-teeth,
Until I find, by you and with you,
  The august, awful destiny.

I saw you yester eve in Fancy's world,
  The best and lovliest thing I could create . .
To-day I hold you as a heaven won,

And have you to my selfish self —
    Lost in you or saved —
As you were th' eternal consciousness !
        To-morrow — what ?
It cannot be without your presence
Preying upon the vitals of my life —
    Further I dare not question :
To-morrow is loving Death's and Life's,
        The idiot's oblivion . .
        The ———

MADGE.

O thy presence, Madge, is sprinkled deep,
With the quick stars of delight,
The flowers of sense and song and sleep,
Symbols of beautiful might ;
Dost thou know sweet Madge that the little white laugh
And whispers of love-caught girls,
Are nestled low in the toils I quaff
Of thy silken, odorous curls ?

O thy touches, Madge, are electric sparks
From the pulses of leaping love,
Thy ways and words are saving arks
That bear to the storied above ;
Dost thou know, bright Madge, that thy velvety feet,
Thy heart-hand and hand of fire,
Are coated hard with the liquid sweet
Of summer and soft desire ?

O thy beauty, Madge, burns low and wide,
And thy joyous smiles leap high,
As the star-lit waves of a silver tide,
To the throne of a star-made sky;
Dost thou know, dear Madge, that the rapture rife,
And the sunshine round thy way,
Are the mellow beams of thy golden life,
And reflections of thy day?

NINA MAY.

THOU exceptional creation,
Nina May,
O thou witching inspiration,
Nina May,
What with thy dear eyes' confession,
Thrilling, eloquent confession,
Lives there a more sweet obsession,
Niña May?
Has all earth one such expression,
Nina May?

There's noon sunshine in thy glances,
Nina May,
That my waiting soul entrances,
Nina May,
Claiming Virtue's purest praises,
Wooing Beauty's truest praises,

Lifting from Life's tangled mazes,
    Nina May,
Thy glance warms the soul it raises,
    Nina May.

Then they bless, these ministrations,
    Nina May,
All thy witching inspirations,
    Nina May,
Kill the leaden cares of living,
Each unhappy round of living,
With a sure command achieving,
    Nina May,
Thy glad lover's glad thanksgiving,
    Nina May.

WRITTEN IN AN ALBUM.

A NAME penned on a fading page,
  A name drawn on the drifting shore,
May live a little empty age,
  Then be the blank it was before;
But who engraves upon the mind
  Some darling deed or bless-ed thought,
Shall grasp the happy arts that bind,
  And win the deathlessness he sought.

TO MINE OWN.

THEY say earth's scenes are glad and gay,
And joyance give,
To the quick visions' every ray,
And alway live;
But my eyes know
Naught of the show,
Why should they not refuse to see,
When filled by thee?

They say there's music in the air,
From sea to shore,
Sweet chords re-echoed everywhere,
Thus, evermore;
But none I hear
However near,
How can my ears bring such to me,
When filled by thee?

They say there's Pleasure to be wooed,
A queenly queen,
Whose charms forever are renewed,
Thus, ever green ;
Yet, tho' so loved,
Me hath not moved,
How can my heart another's be,
When filled by thee ?

JULIET.

MY love was born of the womb of hate,
  Alas ! for a love thus sadly born,
Alas ! for the mark of a barren fate,
  And the cloud that darkened my rosy morn ;
That hate — half lovely for love's sake —
  The parent hate slew its offspring love,
But not 'till the martyred thing did make
  Its fate a rebuke of the curse that strove :
Love's breath like a stream of the setting sun,
  Sweetened my veins to my finger tips,
And when our amorous day was done,
  Each died on the other's poisoned lips.

CONTEMPLATION ON THE UXMAL RUINS.

APPROACH and pause — there is a feeling here
That stifles words and half provokes a tear;
That comes abroad with wonder overcast,
And coldly points to a mysterious past;
Like to some jewels rare whose each bright face
Doth mock the poor dead fingers they encase,
Or dungeon's gloom that here and there hath won
A stream of light from some far-distant sun —
So these strewn fragments pour their pregnant rays,
And speak of distant worlds and mightier days,
Of vast conditions with their human seas,
Of golden cities and voluptuous ease,
When was the pile that now such sadness wings
The awe of peoples and the pride of kings.

And such the fall that even nations know,
The gilt of thrones at best a fleeting show;
Thus Life and Death by Time are borne along,
Reactions each of Virtue and of Wrong;

Pause then and weep — the place is all a grave,
The sepulchre of sovereign and slave ;
Here pride and state resolve to humble dust,
The toys and tools of luxury and lust,
And power that erst could dazzle and dethrone,
Resigns its sceptre to a crumbling stone.

Is this the finis then of human might,
And this the fall from man's remotest hight,
Proud man who loves his filmy waifs to flaunt,
Replete with his own littleness and want?
Approach, vain god, and scan this empty scroll !
And earthiness behold thy earthy goal,
The consummation of a common lot,
Alike dismembered — and alike forgot.

Ah, this is not the all of human strife,
'Tis but a page and not the book of life !
Oh ! God of Law ! we bless thee for the text
That makes this world a preface to the next !
A pilgrimage of one short day and night,
An infant school, a fledgling's trial flight,
Where Sense can catch a taste of Heaven's sea,
And Mind a glimmer of the vast to be,
Yet store each deed and thought from very birth
In the great garner of immortal worth.

IMMORTALIA.

IMMORTALIA.

If a man die shall he live again?

WHO shall dare say — *sing no more*,
And put a limit to the Voices?

. . .

All the seas shout ceaselessly,
The thousand oceans will not be hushed;
The feathered sparks of the air sing,
And the winds empty their iron lungs,
Battling with hoarse-throated thunders;
Music vibrates throughout the worlds,
The chorus-pulse of universes,
Leaping electrically —

. . .

Who says sing no more
Is the laughter of the All-mind of all space,
And the untiring missionry of Life.

Time — a slight link in eternity —
Shall have her ways perfected
So sure as God is !
God-Man, hungering for repletion,
Forever hungering and acquiring,
Yet never satisfied — nor can be.

The end is but the phantom of a lie,
And a myth's ghost . .
The ring upon a maiden's finger
May well rebuke such ignorance to shame,
Or voices from the burning-bush of Conscience,
The stings of Memory or the sweets of Hope.

O, glory in the works of the Great Now,
The quick compensation of good works,
The waiting tribute of unfolding knowledges,
The ready and magnificent reward
That all things bear within themselves —
. . .
But he is mad who dares limit these
To the poor span and atom of mortality . . .
. . .
The flame-like and everlasting Thought,
That from the canvass or the quarry leaps,

The poet's page, the sage's porch,
The sublime womb whence livid Music springs,
Shall not in the grand economy of things
Fall fledglings in half-spent existence,
But shall break unto Beauty and Perfection,
Spanning the grave as though it were not,
And with electric bound
Grasp the divine glory of full growth,
And fill the worlds with vital splendor.

And that which men call Crime,
The unripe fruit that Life bears,
Nurtured by Society —
Shall ripen in the garden of men's lives . .
Or like foam-flowers
Follow — a yeasty Nemesis — in their wake,
'Till they be brought to smooth and full fruition,
And mingle with the common sea of good . .
Nor shall re-birth to other worlds
Stay the sublime procedure.

We lie in our very names of things —
Finite!
Who dares say it grovels in the dark,

And knows nor God nor Destiny!
Break down the thin-air veil of flesh,
The gossamer wall we name mortality,
And gaze upon the Boundless Wonder!
The deep white Mystery!
The confounding Infinite!
Away with creeds and tome-bound codes,
Or the free thought that is the slave of slaves —
Look, and shrink back appalled!
Then dare invent a limit to the Limitless,
Or seek to weigh the Universal God!

There *is* no Finite!
The vast weird mysteries of space,
Strange suns and systems,
Exchanging forms with neighbor worlds,
Or in the glorious economy
Contributing to new,
Are of the indestructible Eternal. .
Nor less the gentler particles of God,
Great in their diminution. .
. . .
The very atoms of an infant's breath
Type forth the everlasting law!

Ah, the quenchless Memory,
And the soul of things!
If *your* Lord's universe shall die,
Not so the leaf beneath my glass,
Or the master brute
Swinging upon my eye-lash. .
A lover bestowed a dead flower in Thebes —
It was *not* dead!
Its fragrance led a soul through wildernesses,
And saved a thousand years' suffering. .
A bird upturned a dozen goblets of gall,
And when the falconer is enthroned,
So will the bird be. . .
O shout aloud
Ye silver drops tinkling from stalactite;
The chorus of gad-flies and bee-hummings,
White-sand-songs,
And ripple-melodies, shall be sure strains
In the growing music of undying souls. .

. . .

You saw a foot-print in the sand — and wept-
Steal from the thunder-seat of Jove,
And learn the immortality of a tear!

* * * * * *

And love's wild victory is won,
And I am exalted to a Worshiper—
For I have found what glory is to life,
And the ways of magnanimity. .
Henceforth I am a doer of day-deeds,
For my knowledge has solved the things of night,
And made me free as thought.

To be a Beauty-Worshiper — is enough,
A crucible of endless impulse,
Magnetic inspiration,
Quick and more clean than whetted fire,
Purifying as it lifts the soul. .
The only Savior that my Being craves,
And sweet Proclaimer of eternity.

Because of thee, dear thing, I bless my being. .
For with a power as strong as chains —
Yet chainless —
Thou bindest me to Life's appreciation,
'Till blessing is the atmosphere I breathe ;
Through thee my kind and lesser kinds I bless,
The all Resplendent God !
The Infinitesimal Infinite !
For all is pregnant with thy vital sweetness,

And thy unfolding Deity,
And I bless all and thereby am I blessed.

* * * * * *

I know whereof I speak,
For I have peered beyond the veil of earth,
And touched the future pulses ;
Communed in patient watchings,
By long sufferance and the canker,
With Life's fore-runners,
And Heaven's pioneers. .
Felt the angelic kiss and breath-dew,
The embrace of coming worlds,
With their hard warmth and actuality ;
Drank burning prophecies from olden lips,
Felt, saw and know,
O, know the heavenly Reality,
The *only* Real!
Man lives! man lives again!

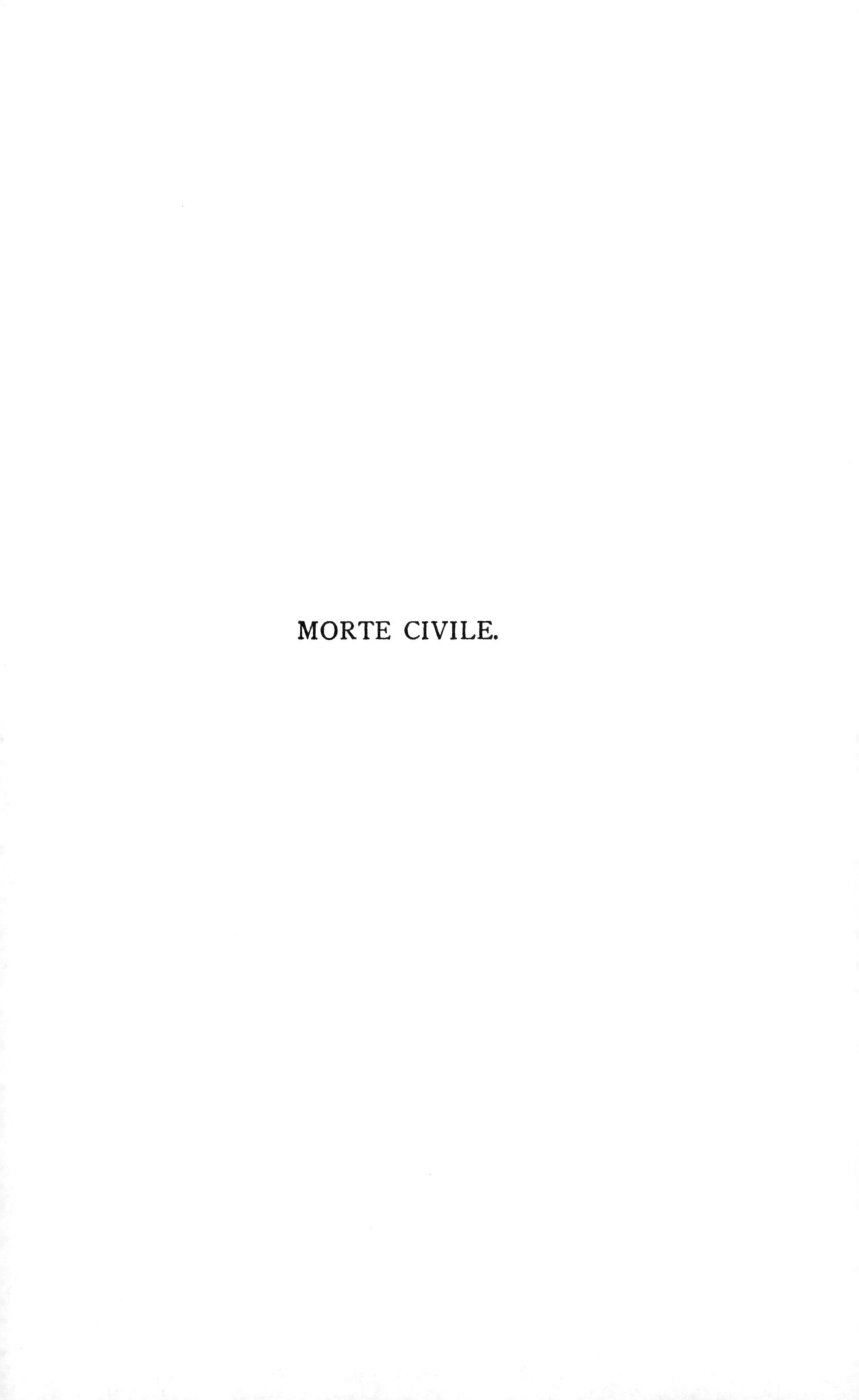

MORTE CIVILE.

MORTE CIVILE.

THE Nemesis of Shame pursues the hour,
The hour we deem so dizzy in its hight ;
Mocked by the perjured privilege of power,
Our boasted splendor wears the stain of night ;
And Justice weeps o'er her rejected dower,
And hides the heaven of her holy might,
Stayed is the flow of Mercy's pregnant shower,
Veiled the illume of Wisdom's willing light,
Lo, God-like courage skulks in guilty cower,
And gory hands applaud the prostrate form of Right.

* * * * * *

Upon life's highway when the sun was high,
With youth and hope their only heritage,
Two good hearts met, t' exchange the tattling sigh,
That glad provoked to love's impelling rage . .
And silver-throated bells with bells did vie,
In loud re-echo of the joyous page,
When did immortal love and constant faith engage.

And Time sped on his over-jocund way,
And blessed the union with a lavish hand;
Three blooming children came to raise their day,
As happ'ly high as Bliss may dare command;
But like a palace builded on the sand,
Uptorn and wrecked by Fates at wanton play,
Death came to show their heaven the havoc of his sway.

A wine thirst seized the lover-husband's breast,
By want and wanton injury inflamed;
It came the fatal robber of his rest,
Spurring his conduct like a beast's untamed;
Poor slave! he was not willingly possessed
By this fell demon that his peace had maimed,
By this red serpent that his being claimed,
Nor power had he to crush th' intrusive guest,
Nor strongly stay the foe that bowed his fated crest.

One night — the darkest of his mortal race —
When vanquished in the battle of the bowl,
A loser in the life-destroying chase
Of passions ere they reach their gory goal,
He tottered forth to work his deep disgrace;
He staggered forth to stain his blotless soul.
Let the deep night preserve the whited scroll!

But lo ! his arm unconscious of its trace,
Has wrought a deed of death that night cannot efface.

Ah, now indeed was he misfortune's child,
Hotly pursued by Fate's too willing whip ;
Deep on his head were eager fetters piled,
Damn'd to the bone by ev'ry venomed lip ;
Twelve erring men, the saints of Justice styled,
Who dared in human blood their hands to dip,
And stamp its stains upon their jury-scrip. .
Outpour, anon, their judgments weak and wild,
And grasp the trembling wretch with their unhallowed grip.

Now closed about the prisoner's awful doom,
And Death's grim visions gorged his aching eyes ;
He felt the terrors of a gaping tomb,
Whose freezing silence mocked his burdened sighs ;
But not unshared did he his griefs assume —
Proclaim her virtue to th' applauding skies !
Close by his side, despite the preying gloom,
A true wife weeps her fertile sympathies ;
Anon, despairs more vast and darker loom,
More warm, apace, her sacred ministries,

More loud to Mercy her imploring cries,
From the last depths of woe's mysterious womb,
Or wildly reaching forth to Hope's sublime illume.

But lo ! a flaw is hunted from its lair !
Who dared to blunder o'er a human life ?
Unveil the rash and over-lusty slayer,
Who makes a plaything of this awful strife :
Shall ignorance become the hangman's knife ?
The page from out the nation's record tear —
Is not enough of blood and madness rife ?
God's creature bartered for a simple care !
Vain now their loud regrets, 'tis done beyond repair.

The twelve rash men have done — they know not what —
A verdict drawn to be in part undone,
Dependent on a gov'nor's flighty thought,
Who might be human or a flinty stone ;
But lo ! the hero's name with hope is fraught,
For many a great and gracious fight he's won .
'Give grateful tidings to this prostrate one,
I will that he shall have the life he's sought,
Now ring it high and far this holy deed I've wrought.'

And it *was* rung — afar and near 'twas rung —
Th' impatient wires quick bore it through the land
And made a theme for ev'ry eager tongue ;
And men rejoiced that Hate's vindictive brand
Had into Pity's cooling wave been flung. .
But she, the weeper — he o'er whom then hung
Death's stern and dark and terrible demand,
How may *their* joy — last joy — be told or sung ?
Oh how divinely strong this saving hand !
How trebly sweet high Mercy's liquid lung,
That yields a vintage full of blisses warm and young.

But like a damn'd assassin in the night,
Who gives a torch but bids it light to death,
Or a false guide with whom is scaled a hight
Where 'stead of heaven he grants a hell beneath,
So came this magnate's triply poisoned breath,
So came the crushing of this wild delight ;
His knife he stayed more keenly to unsheath,
His respite only veiled a bloodier sight,
His mercy curbed a blow to bring a deadlier blight.

Bring forth the pale and trembling pris'ner now,
The fickle magnate bids that he shall die ;

Lead forth the man whose wet and pallid brow
But now was Life's refreshed and roseate sky ;
And tell him ere his senses duller grow
That he's the victim of a legal lie,
And mock him if he dares to question why ;
Aback ! and let the red lord have his show !
O could some power compel him nearer by,
That he might easier see the life-blood flow,
And hear the broken heart's despairing cry,
And know the floods of tears that he disdains to dry.

* * * * * *

Lo ! it is done ! the deed of death is done !
Deliberate and passionless and cold !
The civil sands have had their black hour's run,
The tale of Godly murder has been told —
A Hydra's, and no single serpent's fold,
Has grappled human life then crushed the prize it won.

Behold the trophies of a Christian age !
The shadows of a night both dark and fell,
When Mind was but the seat of Hate and Rage,
Here made the echo of the same dread knell . . .
Oh ! tear it from Life's better, truer page,
The tooth for tooth that is the law of hell.

APHRODITIS.

APHRODITIS.

A PASSION MONODY.

WHO hath become *as one of us* in love-lore,
The deeps of love-sighs having sounded,
And proved the travail of her pulses,
Inspired unto the mysteries of bliss?

O, Woman! type of beautiful divineness!
Th' incarnate rapturous Cause art thou,
Astarte, Juno or the Ark of worlds!

I worship God in this strange worship,
And feel his vivid gloriousness;
His sharp breath touching my life-strings,
The creamy breast that is his breast,
With its generous palpitations of white heaven,
Blessing with magnetic nourishment.

And if it be a bitter thing — yet will I love,
And weep in Love's Gethsamene,

Rising on wild wings of freedom,
  Sanctified, renewed and strong,
  In sovereign resignation.

I am most happy when having most of love,
  And I have most of love when I love most;
It is the truth that shall redeem the world —
  Possession in proportion as we give,
  Enlightenment as we enlighten,
  Salvation in the ratio that we save,
The soul's own compensation in its works —
  The key to blissful immortality.

Bright inspirations touch my line of life
          Like jewels on a star-path ;
  Una or undying Florina,
Yolonde, Urline, Ælæa or Glaphira —
'Tis a communing with my greater self,
        As stars do with their suns —
My soul-wife, the feminine of my being,
My counterpoise unto a balanced whole. .
  Her influence is a scented spell,
That steals unto the subtlest depths of me,

Till I am lost in sweet duality,
And doubly know my blest completeness;
Her lighted eyes, with mine, peer doubly deep,
Catching the full sublimity of things;
Our words are wedded;
Our touches leap in magnetic marriage;
The dual heart converts the dual will,
Till it be quick to harmony;
And by the breath's incense do we worship,
And all emotions are of Beauty,
And every sense interprets Peace and God.

I know no being mightier than this,
Loving, and being loved;
For it woos forth all grossness from our lives,
And sanctifies them unto golden truth;
It is the link between myself and kind —
This woman-worshiping —
A covenant between my Lord and me,
That, charm-like, draws me heavenward.

And, Oh, confide with ample confidence;
Thy trust is darling as my eye's pupil,
And sacred as the chamber of my God;
True unto thee is true unto myself,

And th' divine majesty of my light,
That cannot lead astray ;
Thy faith shall make thee whole as Beauty is,
And lead thy soul, through me, to happiness,
And Love's exalted adorations.

Never, my soul-life, can I let thee go,
For I have tasted of thy sweet infinity,
And felt the delicious burnings of thy breath
Baptise me unto ecstasy ;
Thy warm life floods me with its spell
Like a new sun !
And in its potent emanations
I find the sacred ravishments of time,
And know the blessedness of sweet content.

Were I to lose thee, fair Creatress,
Then would I understand decay,
And the cold ways of barren famine ;
I think it better that I had not been . .
Else fashioned for no other thing
Than the mere jest and minute-toy of Fate ;
What though with fertile weeping
I irrigate the desert left to me,
Yet whence the warmth and pregnant light
To woo one blank oasis into bloom,

Even of a grave's measurement?
Nay thou fount of all my Nile of life,
I must have thee and partake of thee
As thou wert the very end of things,
Or key to where no end can be;
And I will hold thee by Love's chains
That fasten where thy soul is deepest;
And by Devotion's singleness
That charms thee heaviest
With incense of its alters,
Till we are inter-wed like wine floods,
And have but one identity.

O slay me with thy kisses' scythe, beloved;
Thy kisses that are warm and heavenly moist,
Conveying vintages more stinging sweet
Than all th' distilled flowers of mother Earth;
Thy presence, mine, is quick with joyousness,
And th' weird prophecies of the Infinite;
There is no marvel that I cling to thee,
And have thee to my finger-tips;
My consciousness is full of thee,
Unto my soul's fastnesses;
Thou art a shrine freighted with miracles,

And he must yield who would be God-bound ;
Thou art my bearer of the lighted Truth ;
For the Beautiful has set us free,
And the heart conveys the head to majesty,
And Arcana of exalted happiness.

Pry'thee, beloved, be not too near to me ;
Thy touch is keen as lightning's knife,
That cleaves the pale heart of night,
And leaves it trembling in wild wonderment ;
Even the soft tinseling thou wear'st
Is instinct with strange quickness,
Like spirit feet upon thin brittle glass,
In telegraphy to its soul — to break !

. . .

The ring, see, has cut clean to th' bone ;
So these pregnant flowers thou gavest me,
Taught by thy vital breath to breathe,
Thou knowest not they burn and scald like fire . .
Howbeit their color is of blood — my blood !

. . . . . .

Thy presence is a perfume, lovely thing,
And when thou sighest with thy tender soul,
Or sham'st the diamond with thy jewel tear,

Thou fill'st the world with thy crushed fragrance,
  And I smell thy sacred sweetness to my depths;
Thy breath's dews are as spirit wine,
And I drink thee — sharper than the gods' armita,
  'Till I'm renewed by angel healing,
And praise my God, through thee, for my sublimity.

Or speak — and a fountain stream tinkling
  O'er stalagma is thy music speech,
And beautiful as the path of the white fawn
  Traced out by sun-lit flowers;
And I am as thou'lt have me; thy tongue's convert,
  And convert of thine eyes I am;
And I yield unto thy eloquence with worship,
  Crying amen — and yet amen — to thee.

* * * * * *

Great souls love not as the low orders love;
  Brute life is true to its development,
  Be so the higher Mind to his;
And let the emanations from Man-hood,
  In deed and word and presence,
Be noble as God's seal within it set,
  And mirror forth the everlasting light.

THE SYLPH-DREAM.

THE SYLPH-DREAM.

IN the spring-time, I remember,
On a beauty-haunted night,
Still as slumbering September,
Mant'ling skies besprinkled bright,
When the moon I well remember
Filled the world with mellow light,
I reclin-ed by a brooklet;
By a runnel sweetly ringing,
By a rillet softly singing,
And about all else was sleeping,
Save the stars all else was sleeping,
And they, through the foliage peeping,
Seemed to say,
In their way,
That Love's vigils they were keeping,
Night and day.

And I slept there, couched on flowers,
Laden with Aroma's dowers,
  From the stores of honey-homes,
Hid in cups 'neath tiny domes,
Or entranced beneath the showers
Beauty gave to fill the bowers,
Charm-ed else by kissing hours,
    There most happily I lay;
But the moments small in number
Passed me bound in empty slumber;
        Soon above me,
        As to love me,
  There appeared a floating form,
And with laughing pleasure beaming,
Most delightful was the seeming,
  Of the white and fleecy form;
And he bended kindly o'er me,
As a friend he bowed before me,
  Though unknown his incantations;
For he seemed some god of magic,
And in nature gay and tragic,
  His electrical creations;
But he did not come with sadness,
  Nor to bring me troublous dreams,

For his smile was filled with gladness,
  And his eye with darling themes,
      And a peace ;
Then he seemed no child of madness,
    But a Morpheus of peace.

And I 'woke — not from reposing,
Passive as a lakelet's dozing —
But found out the inner seeing
Of the soul's untrammeled being ;
And with strange allurements laden,
  And of Beauty's rarest mould,
There appeared a sylph-like maiden,
  In a beam of Titan's gold.

And she rose up chaste and queenly,
  Jeweled-clothed it seemed to me,
Rose up pensively, serenely,
  Soft as Aaron from the sea —
      And go find
      In any wind,
Though the sea its charms surrender,
  One to vie of womankind
With this vision sweet and tender.

*   *   *   *   *

Lo, anon, th' illusion vanished !
And confusion's clouds unfurled,
And my eager gaze was banished
By the goddess of the world,
As its charms were too transcendent
Viewed so void of preparation,
Not then mine to know contentment,
Filled to sweet intoxication,
And each ray
Quick stole away,
Like Astræa, to heaven.

Strangely mocking were the feelings
Then possessed my prostrate frame,
Wrought as by a demon's dealings,
Or an evil spirit's game ;
Uninviting visions bound me,
Fell contesting clouds around me,
Gloom and thunders to confound me,
And discordant rudeness came,
Forms ungainly to astound me,
Without character or name,
That like unsubstantial surges
On the sea's tormented shore,

With uncertain, broken dirges,
  Came and went to come no more.

Thus when — some deep Wrong deploring -
  Battle comes with stern alarms,
Though Death loves her red outpouring,
It is well, for 'mid her roaring
  Justice breathes in Freedom's arms ;
As when angry Winds are raging,
  With the Element's unchained,
There is in the wild engaging
  Mighty lessons to be gained,
As in Tempests there is Power,
  E'en through Death a Power to save,
As, although in dread they tower,
  There is Virtue in the Wave,
As in Rains and Floods destructive,
  There is gracious Life sustained,
In the Lightning's flash reductive ;
  A Divinity proclaimed,
  So in this there was a Good ;
In the visions strange that bound me,
In the clouds that fell around me,
In the thunders to confound me,
  Were a Wisdom and a Good.

But for shadows' stern appearing,
We would lose our love for light;
Day be robbed her joy endearing,
If unbalanced by the night.

If we knew nor cross nor sorrow
Upon life's short-spann-ed way,
It would be a dead to-morrow,
All unfertile as to day.

'Tis the pain of separation
That makes union's bliss replete,
And the pangs of degradation
Our prosperity so sweet.

When below our course is ended,
Though with sad experience trod,
Better, for such woes transcended
Will we know the place of God.

Lo! again delight dispenses!
Night again by day is chased,
And the scene that charmed my senses
With its splendors, is replaced;

And its sheening,
Wore a seeming,
Like a star with silver traced ;
Like a star-queen's shining dwelling
Stained with jewel-sprinkled gold,
When Delight's glad tales were telling,
As rich Beauty's had been told ;
Like a moon-lit, joy-lit valley,
When bright Luna brightest beams,
And her staff of stars all rally
To o'erlook its glassy streams ;
Like a sphere of sunny story
Sung beneath Enchantment's spell ;
Like a world of God-lit glory,
Or a diamond-lighted dell ;
Like the grots of sparkling dream-land,
When sweet smiles with smiles do vie,
Like the courts of the unseen-land
When unnumbered suns are high ;
Like the homes of olden lustre,
Loves of the Hesperides,
Gardens fair of golden lustre,
Groves of the Hesperides.

And again appeared that being!
Bringing pleasure
Without measure,
Breast and brain at once agreeing,
That heaven contained no richer treasure.

Ah! she was a child of brightness,
Purest joy her lingering wove,
In her soul's unshadowed whiteness,
All an element of love;
All a mind of modest 'havior,
All an image of the blest,
All to seem a virgin-savior,
All a minister of rest,
All to nominate emotion,
All a messenger of light,
All a mirror of devotion,
All an archetype of right;
There was gladness gladly beaming
In her smile so blandly streaming,
And her look was all redeeming,
All compassionate and kind,
And delights about her teeming,
Could no purer presence find.

But the grandest was the soul-sense . .
O its brightness — its omnipotence !
As if Light and Love were married
  In the chambers of that eye,
At the time when Beauty tarried
  With her sunny graces nigh.

And I looked with gaze enchanted,
  Fixed, unwearied and intense,
All content, yet uncontented,
All composure, yet suspense ;
Then how gladly had I parted
With the world, the chilly-hearted,
  With this night of violence —
All things mortal seemed intrusive,
Unsubstantial and illusive,
  So entranced were soul and sense !

  Now a scene unmarked before
  Addressed my senses with its store —
'Twas a summer mold by moon-light,
Now as bright as if by noon-light,
  And I saw a youth reclining
  On a brooklets's mossy lining,

By a runnel sweetly ringing,
By a rillet softly singing,
And with him all else was sleeping,
Save the stars all else was sleeping,
And they through the foliage peeping
Seemed to say,
In their way,
That Love's vigils they were keeping,
Night and day.

Toward the youth were now directed
With a gaze gods would aspire,
Those rich eyes that had subjected
All about with their soft fire ;
Oh ! how envied I the dreamer,
Though I tried it to repress,
For I could not help but deem her
One whose very look could bless ;
And behold she does address him,
Parts those peerless lips nectarian,
And in measures of Arion,
Thus most happ'ly doth address him.

"On a bough that gently wrestles
With the zephyrs of a mead,

Is a flower and in it nestles
  An undying tiny seed.

"In a vale where gaily skipping,
  Joyous birds unlisted sing,
From a thymy covert dripping,
  Is a still, perpetual spring.

"In a mountain's heart unquarried,
  Sleeps a rock low down and dark,
And in its flinty core deep buried,
  Is a small but quenchless spark.

"Like to the spark, and spring, and seed,
  Young slumbering wight art thou ;
An individual, only reed,
  Which fills the eternal Now.

"Like to the seed, and spark, and spring,
  Is a bursting soul like thee,
A frenzied flood, yet a fragile thing,
  A drop of the shoreless sea.

"Like to the spring, and seed, and spark,
  O g'orious moth thou art,

A crater's source or a nation's ark,
And still but an atom part.

"But beware! thou trusting thing, beware!
For a labyrinth is the earth,
Thy virtue guard with a burning care,
And be jealous of thy worth.

"The seed may grow a gnarl-ed thing,
And with cold dead fruit abound,
About which creeping poisons cling,
A cumberer of the ground;
Or it may spread a noble form,
Be grand and stately styled,
With sinews that can mock the storm,
The monarch of the wild.

"The spring may grow a swollen flood
And o'erleap its proper bed,
Drunken and mad with th' wines of blood,
A monster of death and dread—
Or it may flow a lordly tide,
Flow the darling of the land,
Upon whose bosom riches ride,
To bless each prosp'ring strand.

"The spark may burst with fiendish glare
To a conflagration's waste,
Filling with death or deep despair
Where its Ætnean breath has passed,
Or it may rise with a joyous blaze
To an even nourishing flame,
With eternal life in its golden rays,
And eternal hope in its name.

"Choose then youth an immortal choice,
To-day must thou make thy leap !
Thou power hast to make men rejoice,
Or power to make men weep ;
Thou may'st, forsooth, be a giant knave,
Be a monster and disgrace,
Or yet a saint that can shield and save,
And a glory to thy race.

* * * * * *

Lo, herewith ceased the weird strain
That my ravished soul did hear,
And quick as thought can speed the brain
Did the sylph-dream disappear.

PREFATORY.*

LO ! still they come ! one more to swell enough !
 Some poor self-offering for the scribblers' pyre ;
Another fated cries — ' lay on Macduff,'
 And volunteers his head to play the ly-ar ;
Now who again has dared to don rebuff,
 And prays to treat us round with honeyed fire,
Or comes with hair unshorn, or stockings blue,
To tell the world of what it never knew ?

Alas ! that more black oil should be ignited !
 That more winged hoofs should gallopade our airs !
Authors, like duns, come always uninvited,
 Attack our doors and bugle us their wares ;
Thus now an added promise has alighted,
 And with a fertile impudence declares,

*This poem has escaped its intended place as the Preface of the volume.

'Lo! it is I, with latest revelations!'
And here begins to petrify the nations:

Not with delight; O no! but with his daring:
With many words but not with what is in them;
Glass words that have a tissued outer glaring,
But break away as one does only skim them;
And so at last the prize beyond comparing,
Though fit for naught is doubly fit for Hinnom;
Scene second is a subtle irreflection,
Because its ashes fail to pass inspection.

What cannibals do strut a Christian land!
What gibbeting doth innocence inherit;
O what a law that wills a worthy stand,
Not on his feet but always on his merit:
There must in this be something contraband;
At least it shows a sort of hectoring spirit,
Or else there's magic in the critic's school,
That makes a man by making him a fool.

Here is much cause for candid speculation,
To be, or not to be! the case is plain,
Whether 'tis nobler to ignore inflation,
Or be interred nor mourners nor refrain;

I'll leave a will at least for legislation,
Then if I am or am not 'tis the same,
Dub the reviewers, gods! a farewell shamming,
That they, mayhap, may bless me with a dam'ing.

THE END.

www.ingramcontent.com/pod-product-compliance
Lightning Source LLC
LaVergne TN
LVHW011211110826
845150LV00006B/1396

9781425517489